ENDORSEMENTS

I couldn't wait to read Ten Minutes to Live. *Mike and Sheri Schaefer are an example to families everywhere that when bad things happen to good people, there is hope! Sheri tells her story with sincerity and brings you right into the hospital room, just as if you were sitting there with her. I felt as if I was a member of her congregation waiting for the next update and ready to pray. You will feel Sheri's pain, you will experience Sheri's victory, and ultimately you will learn that* Ten Minutes to Live *is proof that all things are possible. This book is for anyone going through a difficult time, especially those facing a medical crisis.*

— Dr. Leslie McNulty, Cofounder
Christian Adventures International

Your eyes have fallen upon a beautiful love story told in the face of darkest night. It is a journey of faith and love crowned with triumph and hope. Witnessing this family overcome this trial was to behold the beauty of the Lord's unfailing love worked out in real life. Imbibe deeply and drink slowly from this well. You will be inspired and encouraged as you learn that we are not helpless when partnering with God in the battles of life and death. Mike and Sheri have blessed us by their unwavering faith in our ever-present Father.

— D. Alan Hawkins, D. Min., Pastor
New Life City

In Ten Minutes to Live, *Sheri Schaefer gives us the blueprint on how to be victorious during times of great trials. Starting with a firm foundation, built over her years of trusting in God's Word, Sheri begins by refusing to let blame and guilt divide her family. using all the advantages of a Spirit-filled believer, she counters any words of doubt, unbelief, and disunity with the harmony of unceasing prayer and faith-filled confession. Her love for her husband, her children, and their families, her church, and her fellow believers is a testament that the words of 1 Corinthians 13:13 were always in the center of her being: "And now abideth faith, hope, love, these three; but the greatest of these is love."*

— Bob Thorsen, President
Bob Thorsen Construction

So often when faced with tragic situations, the people who love us the most are overwhelmed by the magnitude of the problem. They hear the terrible prognosis and simply repeat the words of physicians over and over, which undercuts their faith in God to intervene supernaturally. Sheri led the fight of faith for Mike's life with such wisdom so others could follow. I believe this book will encourage so many others!

— Cindi Townsley, Pastor
Believers' Center of Albuquerque, New Mexico

If you've ever questioned God's provision for your life, or even found yourself in a position of questioning your own faith in God, Ten Minutes to Live *is the key to unlock the God-given strength you never imagined existed within yourself. As Sheri and her family demonstrate their unwavering love for God and each other in the midst of painful experiences, you will learn how to stand when you're faced with the storms of life. God's faithfulness to his Word* and the power in it resounds throughout this book—one that is a true inspiration to us all.

— Cindy Mansfield, Station Manager KNAT-TV/ SW
Regional Manager, Trinity Broadcasting Network

I encourage you to read this life-changing story by Sheri Schaefer. It will inspire you to take God at his Word and believe he is a miracle working God. Mike and Sheri are living examples of this truth.

— Sandy Scheer, Pastor
Guts Church, Tulsa, Oklahoma

Ten Minutes To Live *is an outstanding, fascinating, and true story of how prudent people respond to tragic circumstances. I have known Mike and Sheri Schaefer intimately since 1983, and was one of the friends that received an urgent out-of-state call to pray for Mike's life. If you believe God's unfailing Word and do what they did, you may have the same outcome. It is no coincidence that their church is named Church Alive!*

— Rev. Robin J. Roberts, Founder
Robin Roberts Ministries

What a great story Ten Minutes to Live *is! Sheri Schaefer has put an amazing journey into an easy-to-read book filled with faith, hope, and love. It is a tremendous testimony of what it is to trust God in some of life's most challenging times. The good news is that God is no respecter of persons, and what he's done for Mike and Sheri—as it is so beautifully detailed in this book—he will do for us all, as we keep our trust and abide in a loving Father.*

— Rev. Tony Cooke, Founder
Tony Cooke Ministries, Tulsa, Oklahoma

TEN
MINUTES
TO LIVE

A STORY OF FAITH AND MIRACLES

SHERI SCHAEFER
WITH SALLY HANAN

TEN MINUTES TO LIVE
A STORY OF FAITH AND MIRACLES

Editing team: Inksnatcher, Joanne Sher, and Gene Koskey
Cover & interior layout/design: Allison Metcalfe Design
Author photo: Jamie Jauriqui Photography
First Edition, 2015
ISBN: 978-0991335046
Publisher: Fire Drinkers Publishing

I dedicate this book to Michael, my quite opinionated and beloved husband of forty-three years. Here's to many more years of intense discussions, Bible studies, late nights, truth, boldness, and joyful bliss.

TABLE OF CONTENTS

ACKNOWLEDGMENTS

I am so grateful for the power of God and his great love for me. I am also thankful for the things I have learned from my spiritual father, Kenneth E. Hagin. Without his timeless writings and teachings on faith and healing, I don't believe I would have understood or have been able to stand on God's word for the healing of my husband. I am also thankful for my family and friends who prayed and encouraged me during the journey. How can I ever say thank you, to all of you, enough?

Special thanks to Gene Koskey for doing the preliminary edits and and final proof on this book for me. Also to Pastor Claudia Moore, who confirmed my idea to write a book about my husband's accident when she said, "So when are you going to write a book about this story?" Also, thanks to Chuck and Ralph for continuing to encourage me to finish the book.

1

THE CALL

"Mom?"

Shaun's foreboding tone reaches my insides and steels my body for what's next.

"Mom, Dad has had an accident skiing and they are going to take him by ambulance to the hospital in Santa Fe."

All my thoughts freeze, but somehow one does not.

"Is he in a lot of pain?"

"Yes. I'm going to put you on with Kathy, the EMT. She'll give you directions to the hospital."

The huge French breakfast we all enjoyed hours earlier starts to revolt. I stand in the cemetery we stopped off at— to see the headstone of Jason's grandmother—and now I can't even read the words on it. In my murky fog, every tree and piece of stone is here yet not here. I'm here but not here. All I can hear is my heartbeat.

"Kathy, can you give him something for the pain?"

"I'll see what I can do."

And then I hang up and kick into automatic pastor's wife mode, because I know what to do in an emergency. I ask people to pray. I call pastors, I call family and close friends, and I stand with my daughter, daughter-in-law, and son-in-law in that graveyard that remembers the dead and ask God for the health and, although I did not know it at the time, the life of my husband of thirty-seven years.

2

CUT OFF

DECEMBER 29, 2009

I'll see Mike soon. What was Shaun's tone like on the phone? Is it serious? Has the EMT given Mike anything for the pain? He has a high tolerance for pain. We need to pray. The prayers flow out of our mouths effortlessly as we entreat heaven.

What will we find out when we get there? Will our pregnant daughter and daughter-in-law, Sarah and Meghan, be okay in a germ-filled hospital setting? Racing, racing. My mind has always tried to stay one step ahead.

I reach the front desk of St. Vincent Regional Medical Center and say the name of my husband, my once-accident-prone man, Michael Schaefer. The girl presses a few buttons and then shakes her head no.

My thumbs grip the underside of the counter. "I'll be in the smaller waiting room. Please call me when he comes in."

She nods and her eyes move to the person behind me.

Up and down the hallway, checking on the girls, prayer filling and leaving my mouth like my breathing—rapid. Twice more I return to the front desk to see if Mike has arrived.

"No," says the girl younger than my own daughter. "I'm sorry."

I'm back to pacing the hall when my phone rings. It's Shaun.

"Mom, he's almost there. Are you in the ER? You really need to be there when they bring dad in."

My breath stops midway.

Jason, my son-in-law, must see something in my eyes. "I'll walk back to the ER with you."

✦ ✦ ✦

Michael Anthony Schaefer – that was his full name – was the cute hasher at the dining hall in the Pi Beta Phi sorority house. It was 1970, and I was walking down the stairs when I noticed Michael's plaid, bell-bottom pants that fit really well and a face that took my breath away. I could feel my body temperature and curiosity rising simultaneously, and in the rush that followed, I can't even remember if I said hi or not in passing. I asked around for days until one of my sorority sisters ended my quest.

Being the strategic type, I devised ways to time taking dishes into the kitchen for when I thought Mike would be ready to leave. Needless to say, this very shy guy from southeast New Mexico and I started dating soon after that, and that cute face filled my sophomore year in college and all the years after it.

· 6 ·

Over those on-again, off-again years, I learned about his many accidents—the time a long three-quarter-inch wide stick jabbed him in the armpit one-quarter inch away from a main artery, his countless broken arms, the rattlesnake bite that could have killed him—and his high tolerance for pain.

✦ ✦ ✦

But this time is different. The gurney squeaks into the examination room with Mike's body on it. He is holding his left arm above his head and groaning loudly in pain. I almost fall onto Jason when I hear that, but his arm steadies me and we wait together as they move Mike's 240-pound body onto the bed. He's crying out in pain, and I grip Jason's arm and will my body to stay upright in spite of the sudden weight that has flooded it.

The men leave the room, the doctor nods, and I walk to the bed.

"Can you get me something for the pain?" His face holds lines of agony I have never seen before.

The doctor speaks over him and looks at Jason and me. "Mrs. Schaefer?" He waits for me to affirm my name. "We think Mike has some broken bones, and probably some broken ribs too, which is why his pain level is so high."

Mike grunts in acknowledgment. "I can't breathe. The pain is awful. Having my arm this way ... makes it easier to breathe."

The doctor keeps talking. "You'll need to take off his wedding ring, because there's a good chance his finger will swell up. We can't give him much for pain until we discover the extent of his injuries."

"I really messed up David's ski day today." Mike keeps

· 7 ·

talking. "Did you make the church deposit? Do we have some sermons on file?"

He's always taken care of things, and now he's still doing it: checking on Shaun's friend David, who was supposed to ski with them all day, church people, a teacher for Sunday morning....

He's going to be okay. I lift his hand and start to twist the wedding ring off his finger, and I think this will not be a permanent thing.

✦ ✦ ✦

Mike was so easygoing, so flexible when we dated. Everything was interesting and worth learning about. Nothing was a big deal. He wanted to know about life, about why he was alive in the particular years we were born into, about who he was, about what he was here to do. Having a father killed in the Korean war when you are only two years old can do that to a man. Not dying from a rattlesnake's bite in the same week another girl your age did can do that to a man. His curiosity led us both.

We went to a tarot card reader in that first year of dating. She sat behind the table in her rented booth and clicked one card after another before us. He took me to a handwriting analyst. We wrote silly things on cards and she held them out from her far-sighted eyes and told us we were meant to be together. I wasn't so sure.

We got to our senior year and we'd meet in the library, where we would whisper beside stacks of books on Eastern religions. On our long walks he would tell me about nirvana and history and the way to enlightenment. He tried to get there faster by taking LSD from time to time, only at 2 a.m. one night his trip took him through the front door of my sorority house, all the way to pushing

· 8 ·

the intercom button so that his LSD-laced broadcast could reach me. Not only did it reach me … it reached every girl in the house. "Sheri, come down here, and if it will make you come a little faster, this is God." I certainly wasn't treating him like God, because I broke up with him over and over through those years.

✦ ✦ ✦

But now I need God to intervene a little faster. My husband is in pain and I want to do something, *anything,* to make him okay right now. The tears have been coming and going, and I'm trying to hold myself together.

"Mr. Schaefer, we need to get you ready for your X-rays, so we're going to have to cut off your ski pants."

"No, no; I'll take them off. You don't need to cut them! My wife only just gave them to me. They were a Christmas present!"

My momentary laugh is a welcome relief. I'm touched by how much that present means to him, even as I shake my head.

The doctor's eyes plead with me. I lift and hold Mike's ring-less hand again.

"Honey, we can get you another pair. You don't need to be moving around. You are in extreme pain right now, and we need to find out what's broken so the doctors can fix you up." For a split second I feel useful, helpful. I have no idea this is the last thing he will remember me saying for thirty days.

We sit in the trauma room with the empty bed, waiting for his X-rays and scans to be finished. I twist my wedding ring around and around the finger that supposedly contains the closest artery to the heart and finally ask the question: "Shaun, what happened up there?"

Shaun runs a hand through his thick auburn hair and takes a breath. "Oh, Mom … we'd taken a few runs and then took the chairlift to the top of the mountain with David. The first few runs that morning I'd almost run Dad off the trail; it's so hard to stay together with me on the snowboard. This time we were coming down a wide trail and I decided to go ahead. I was clipping along pretty fast on the right tree line.

"I cut across the run to cut through a gap in the trees and then I heard Dad yell, 'Watch it,' or something like that. I knew right away something wasn't right. Then I heard David yell, 'Mike!' He yelled again, 'Mike!' David yelled a third time, but Dad still didn't reply. I was running up the slope through the snow and saw Dad lying on his back with his skis still tangled in the tree he hit. He must have been following me and I cut him off …." Shaun shifts his weight on the hard hospital chair and he studies the floor.

I put a hand on his back and keep it there.

"Shaun, you and your dad were doing what you loved to do together—something you have done together for most of your life. We both know you didn't mean to cut him off. We both know that.

"Stay in faith with me here. Don't let guilt or condemnation pull you out of faith in God's Word now. Your dad's going to be okay."

We pull on each other's strength.

Mike's going to be okay. I keep repeating that to myself. *Mike's going to be okay.*

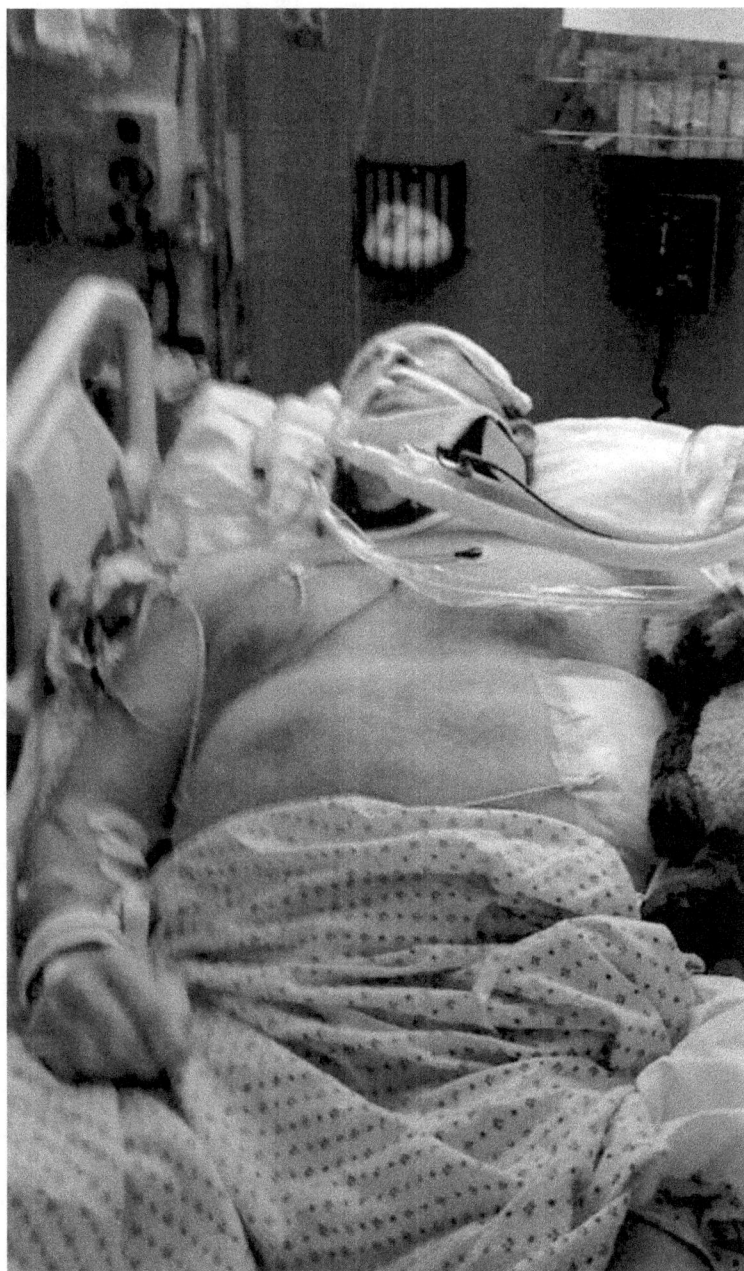

THE DAY AFTER

THE NIGHT BEFORE THE ACCIDENT

· 13 ·

3 GOD'S GOT THIS

But Mike is not okay.

I have watched him come in and out of this room too many times now, and each time he seems to cry louder as they move him from the gurney to the bed. It takes four to six people to move him because of his size. These people care, and they are trying to do this in the most helpful way possible, but each time Mike cries out, my chest hurts.

The fog shrouds me, yet sometimes lifts enough for me to focus on what the doctors are saying. I'm the spectator of someone else's show, with a glass screen for me to look through. I can stay safe on my side. I don't have to feel this. I can just watch. In an hour or two it will be over and I can go back to the life I'm used to living. Any time now.

But now it's 11 p.m. and Mike has been moved to the intensive care unit, because apparently it's not just a simple fall with a few broken bones. He has broken ribs on his left side, and any one of them could puncture his lung. His sacrum is fractured. They are not sure about his kidney function.

I stand outside and do what I have been doing all day—praying in the Spirit, calling more family members and friends. The kids have left for the night, but I want to stay here with Mike. He needs me, and to be honest, I need him. I walk back into the ICU, but a nurse stands in my way.

"I'm so sorry, Mrs. Schaefer, but visiting hours are over for the day." She's so neat and orderly in her hospital scrubs and ponytail, while my insides are tangled up like a very bad hair day.

My first reaction is to push past her. I have absolutely no intention of leaving. I'm not going anywhere—not today, not tomorrow—and don't you dare tell me otherwise! I give her one of my looks, the one that used to work so well on the kids, but her stance is challenging. This is obviously not her first rodeo, so I move to plan B.

"I'd like to speak with your supervisor." I've always lived by a higher authority, and this one should do it.

✦ ✦ ✦

Well ... I wanted to live by a higher authority, but as Mike quickly discovered when we were dating, I was more than happy to have life cater to me, seeing as I was practically an only child because my brother, Dean, was so much younger. Hence the dating, breaking up, dating, breaking up pattern of our relationship. I didn't want to share, didn't want to be flexible, didn't want to accept that I couldn't have my way most of the time. Mike, on the other hand, was used to being part of a loud and boisterous family, with everyone having an opinion at the same time but being very flexible about it.

That senior year, I got tired of seeing Mike not respond to life and to me in the way I expected him to, but I did love him, and I knew what I wanted. I wanted him. It was the seventies, the decade of freedom, so I did what any woman with a will of steel would do: I gave him the "my way or the highway" speech: either marry me after we graduate or break up for good.

✦ ✦ ✦

And now the supervisor is standing in front of me with the same calm "no" in his eyes that I've just encountered in his shorter, female counterpart.

"I'm sorry, Mrs. Schaefer. While I understand your concern and the fact that you want to sit with your husband, we can't change ICU policy. I really do encourage you to go home and rest for the night."

My eyes start to fill. I can feel the wetness rising higher and higher, but I don't want the supervisor to see me like this; I don't want him to think I'll go soft just because he tells me no. I find a tissue in my purse and soak up the vulnerability.

I'm using all of my reasoning powers on him. I'm staying calm and collected. I'm determined.

But it's not enough. I've used up all of my lines and he will not let me through. "I'm not going home. I don't care what you say. I will not leave my husband!"

His shoulders slump. "I can see that you want to stay close, and while again, I recommend you catch up on some sleep, you can rest in one of the waiting rooms tonight if you feel like you can't leave just yet." He moves to head back into the nurses' station, but turns back to me for a moment. "I'll go ahead and check with the nurse to see if you can check in on your husband once or twice in the early morning hours, just for a minute or two."

It's not much, not nearly enough, but that small bit of kindness undoes me again, and the tears blur my path all the way to the waiting room.

I empty about half of the box of thin, hard hospital tissues before I try to maneuver my way into a good sleeping position. *Jesus, you are with Mike as he sleeps. Heal him, Lord. Fill his room with your presence.*

✦ ✦ ✦

Mike didn't know Jesus personally back then, not in the way he does now. His family attended a Roman Catholic church when possible, and all the children were baptized and make their first holy communion, but most Sundays his parents had to take care of the family bar and they couldn't go to church. Mike's parents gave him the space to search, question, experiment, and discover what was real; but even though he had learned what true Christian giving and loving was about, he was still searching.

We talked about God a lot during those college years—his feelings of closeness to God when he spent time in nature or at his aunt and uncle's farm in northern New Mexico; his disillusionment with people never changing, no matter how many times they "confessed"; the prayers he had prayed that went unanswered. As a regular Sunday School attender myself, I knew why Jesus had died, but I wasn't willing to let God tell me how to live my life. In a way we were both searching—wanting more but not quite sure how to get it.

✦ ✦ ✦

I'm still shaking, and from time to time the tears return. Rest is not possible here, alone. Not tonight.

DECEMBER 30

It's 3 a.m., my first sneak peek of the night, and my normally passionate, opinionated man is not fully present. The pain killers have taken over, to a degree. He is lying on his back and I hear a faint "Okay, okay, okay," before his hand smooths the sheet covering him. "Okay, okay, okay," and again his hand lifts onto the sheet and pushes the wrinkles away. If only I could do the same with his accident.

If only I could go back to this time forty-eight hours ago, sleeping next to him after a family walk to the hotel by way of Santa Fe's Basilica of St. Francis—the air tingling on my face and in my lungs, and Mike holding on tight so I won't slip on the snowy sidewalk. He doesn't let go ….

He is fighting for every breath as I watch, and I can only imagine the pain of having to inhale past so many broken ribs.

"Sometimes," a doctor in the ER had said, "we have to intubate a person with this many broken ribs because of the pain involved with breathing. If he can't breathe deeply enough on his own, his lungs can fill with fluid and eventually cause pneumonia." Back then I shook my head no at him, but now I catch the rise and fall of Mike's chest and fear slithers around and in me and begins to petrify my insides.

I am allowed back in at 5 a.m. and two doctors are outside Mike's room. One of them wastes no time.

"We're going to have to intubate your husband."

Air and fear hiss in unison through my mouth and into my lungs.

"His breathing is too shallow and he's not getting

enough oxygen. One of his lungs has collapsed. We have to intubate him to make sure this doesn't continue. His body has started to swell, and it can't cope with the liquid accumulating around his lungs. We have to drain that fluid, and we have to do it as soon as possible.

"Also, his kidneys are failing."

"Can I see him for a moment?"

"Absolutely."

I stand by his bed and stroke his thick hair and kiss his forehead. We lock eyes.

"I love you. You're going to be okay. God's got you." I pray quietly with my hand on his forehead for my "allowed" few seconds and then I have to leave him again.

I can't do this alone. I can't be here alone, and Mike needs backup. I have no idea what's going to happen in the next few hours. I call the kids and let them know they should come back to the hospital ….

"Things aren't good," I tell them. Then I call my prayer partner, Terri; one of our pastors, Becky; Mike's younger sister, Sally Ann (who is in Santa Fe this weekend)— everyone who I know will pray. Lord knows, he needs the covering.

I'm allowed back in once he is intubated.

"Air got in under Mike's skin when we were inserting the chest tube. He is very swollen."

It's just as well they prepared me. I touch the skin on his arm and it crackles and pops like a Rice Krispy. His eyes are almost swollen shut. A wide tube is snaking its way out of his mouth and traveling to a machine that forces air into his lungs in timed sequence. A thinner tube trails out from the side of his chest and down to the collection setup. Mike knows who I am, and in his eyes I can read his message:

"It's okay, Sheri. God's got this."

4 WE WON'T BACK DOWN

I am unaware of what is going on in the spiritual realm during these hours of darkness. Only later will I hear Pastor Marshall's story:

✦ ✦ ✦

It was in the early morning, sometime between 1 and 3 a.m., that I was suddenly made aware of the presence of someone I did not recognize.

I was in a room that had one way in and one way out. Someone, a male figure, stood in the doorway. I was not alarmed by his presence; in fact, I was actually taken more by the atmosphere around me. It was most unusual. I have never experienced anything like it and still struggle for words to describe it. Maybe the word "hollow" or "feigned" is most appropriate.

As I made eye contact with the man, he spoke. In a very pleasant and confident voice he said, "Pastor Mike Schaefer is dead." It didn't seem like an attempt to convince me, just to inform me. No hope was communicated that something might be accomplished to change the situation. No comfort offered, just the news that Mike had died.

Without hesitation, I sensed the Holy Spirit's voice within me to the contrary. Those words so filled my heart at that moment that I could not help but speak them. With great calm and confidence (maybe the gift of faith at work), I said, "No, Pastor Mike Schaefer will live and not die." That was all. "Pastor Mike Schaefer will live and not die." At that exact moment, without argument or delay, the man was gone and the atmosphere in the room changed. I enjoyed an overwhelming sense that all was well.

Then my eyes opened and I checked my surroundings. I remained awake for a while to contemplate what had just happened, to praise God for Pastor Mike's life, and for the move of God to protect him. The next morning, I woke up with a sense that Satan had been trying to find someone to agree with him so that he could end Mike's life. The atmosphere in the room was hollow and empty because the messenger of Satan had carried false words and tried to deliver them as truth. The Holy Spirit in me was able to counteract his lies with God's truth, straight out of Psalm 118:17.

✦ ✦ ✦

Friends are already here and I am adamant about how this will go down, despite my concerns, despite the medical staff saying that things are very serious. I stand in the waiting room with these loyal people.

"We will pray only what the Word of God declares and promises: that Mike is totally whole and healed, and what Satan meant for harm, God will turn around for his glory.

Mike shall not die. Mike shall live. He shall live to proclaim the glorious acts and deeds of the Lord."

They all agree wholeheartedly, and the somewhat heavy atmosphere lifts and drifts out the door. Mike agrees too—he can write on a little whiteboard a nurse has given him, and one pastor shares his recent comment:

Let's kick the devil's butt in Santa Fe.

I am so tired I can barely speak. Hundreds of people are praying. I cannot think of anyone else to notify. The battle is the Lord's. I drive the short distance to the hotel, lay my head on the pillow, and the sandman takes me.

I am back at noon to be with Mike. So many people are here now! Friends, family, church members. Their presence and prayers comfort me throughout the afternoon. Mike's older sister, Paulette, arrives. She says she woke up at 4 a.m. and knew she was to pray for Mike. God reassured her that he is in control and he has a plan for Mike that will be brought to fulfillment.

Before Paulette left for the airport, her daughter told her that she was awakened by a presence in her room that morning that said that Uncle Mike was going to die, but she prayed with her dad and then announced that Mike was going to be all right because he was too stubborn to die. She was right!

Then while Paulette was on the plane here, she had her head down as she was praying, and all of a sudden an angel appeared. It looked just like her grandmother Lulu, but she was all in white and had white feathery wings. Paulette knew her mind wasn't conjuring something up; it was God's way of reassuring her that things were going to be all right. The angel distinctively told her that Mike would be okay, but that it would be a long, hard road to recovery.

More friends share their prayer stories with me. Many, it seems, were awake in the early hours of the morning praying for Mike. They felt the urgency. They are still praying, grouping together in twos and threes to declare life and not death over Mike, and God's healing over his lungs, kidneys, and broken bones.

Mike seems groggier, less communicative. The doctor has upped his pain cocktail. I wonder how he's reacting to the drugs. He was always the mystical one, especially when we were dating.

✦ ✦ ✦

"So what do you think of when you see the stars?"

"Nothing really. They're pretty…. Here, want a drag?"

He would lie there, staring up at the tiny glowing lights that seemed to multiply as he looked for the deeper layers behind them. The drinks, the drugs, the stars—all giving him that spiritual buzz I had no such yearning for. I just wanted to fit in and do whatever other people were doing, which included getting engaged.

Obviously he wasn't feeling the connection I was going for.

✦ ✦ ✦

I stand beside his bed and he's with me but he's not with me, fading in and out of words and reason, fighting the ventilator, and flailing his hand each time he tries. I overhear a nurse's conversation near the bed:

"Three broken ribs … broken bones … kidneys not good."

It's more information than I've had from any medical staff member all day. I scrape my chair loudly in Mike's direction and start reading healing Scriptures over him.

DECEMBER 31, NEW YEAR'S EVE

My insides are moving from simmer to full boil, and I have no intention of turning the gas down. I'm glaring at doctors and watching nurses because I still have not been informed about Mike's original test results, nor am I being updated about his condition every few hours. They've inserted another tube into his side to help drain more of the fluid buildup, yet all I keep hearing from the nurses is that "things are very serious."

My huffing is probably not the most mature way to go about things, but hospitals are supposed to be caring places, and I've been sitting here waiting for the "experts" to do their jobs. Loved ones are supposed to know what's going on and what to expect!

Meghan, my daughter-in-law, leans over in the late afternoon.

"It might be a good idea to find the hospital administration office and find out why no one has told you what's going on."

We walk down together, Meghan with her blooming belly and I with my attitude. We are met with the sight of desk after empty desk and dark silence.

"Hello? Hellooo!"

We hear a chair move way in the back, and then footsteps making their way up to our spot on the floor. He has kind eyes, this man, and he is the unfortunate stand-in for every other admin worker who has gone home to celebrate the

New Year. I breathe a little when I realize this and put my armor down.

"My husband has been in the ICU in critical condition for two days now, and I haven't even had a meeting with a doctor to find out what's happening. I feel like I've had to beg for information, and I still haven't been told much at all."

He finds a pen in the drawer and writes down our information. "I'll get right on this, Ma'am." And he does. We're not even back at the hotel before he calls my phone.

"A doctor will see you and go over everything with you as soon as you come back in."

Mike grew up sharing his opinion. I grew up holding mine in. I think he'd be proud of me tonight.

✦   ✦   ✦

Just like Mike did after our time apart. He hadn't felt capable of committing to the marriage I wanted. We both took trips over the Christmas break so Mike could "think things over," and he faced me in the New Year with his breath held in and his hopes held out.

"I want to get married."

"No you don't! You're just saying it because that's what I want to hear."

"No, I've had a lot of time to think about this, and it's what I want too. I want to marry you."

"Really?"

"Yes, really."

"Well … *that's fabulous!*"

Waiting for us in the ICU waiting area is the hospital CEO—and I realize he's the man I just spoke to at the admin office! Talk about a divine appointment! Shaun and I follow him into the ICU, where he introduces us to one of Mike's doctors, who talks until we stop asking questions. He holds X-ray images up to the glaring screen and points out Mike's eight broken ribs on his left side and one on his right. Then he shows us the fracture in Mike's pelvis and the broken sacrum that will need a pin placed in it at some point. Then he shows us the MRI photos, and we see the small brain bleed at the back of Mike's head. His left lung doesn't have much support due to the broken ribs and has collapsed.

His condition is extremely critical.

Sarah, Jason, Shaun, Meghan, and I make a decision: It doesn't matter what the doctors say the facts are; we are dealing with far more than a physical body. The facts are subject to change, and we will be led by the wisdom of God and speak to every single problem and make it line up with the healing power of God.

All around the building, celebratory fireworks are going off, set by people full of hope for the year to come. We will join with their expectations. If Satan caused this ski accident, then wow! He really had to dig deep to try to find a way past our relationship with God! The devil had to use a tree to try to take Mike out!

We will not back down. In fact, this only makes us more determined to see God's goodness in the land of the living: to see Mike in full health again. We will *not* back down!

LOVE AND SUPPORT FROM FAMILY AND FRIENDS

MEGHAN AND SARAH'S BLOOMING BELLIES

5 YOU WILL NOT STEAL HIS LIFE

Someone has brought me a pale pink bundle of velvet petals and thorns wrapped in film. An elastic band around the stems attaches a packet of powdered food so they do not die before their time. Fitting…

I lift them to my nose and go back in time to a day full of beauty and happy memories in a rose garden—our wedding.

✦ ✦ ✦

The flowers leaned toward us with all their petals and leaves proclaiming their congratulations as I walked back down the aisle with Mike on my arm and his ring on my finger.

He was nervous about getting married right up to the end, or should I say, the beginning. He made it through those days of planning and picking wedding gifts with persistence and a daily marijuana habit I didn't join him in until the weekends. But he still had doubts, until eventually they were calmed by a dream that reassured him that things were going to be okay, and they were. Our day and lives together were trimmed in lace and roses.

✦ ✦ ✦

I take the roses as a sign, even though I waved aside his dream all those years ago. And I am unaware of the dreams he is experiencing now.

✦ ✦ ✦

MIKE

I remember several different scenarios in my dreams and visions. The theme was the same in all of them: I was struggling to survive. For example, in one vision I saw myself in a Mexican city with a young Mexican lady looking to help me, but in the next, I was alone on a street and had been with guys dealing drugs. I felt an overwhelming sense of helplessness. I was in a wheelchair with no money. I didn't know the language, no one wanted to help me, and the gangsters were looking for me.

There was one vision, though, that produced much peace: In one scene I saw a group of people from many nations praying for me. In the next scene, I was in the wilderness beholding a black wolf and an eagle. The wolf represented endurance (it can go long periods without eating), and the eagle represented strength and victory (soaring above the problems). I was facing a very trying time in the scene. I was crying out for help, and the people who were supposed to be taking care of me seemed to totally ignore me. I felt I was dying, but as with the wolf's endurance, the idea that continued to spring from my mind was *I will not die*, and what came from my heart was, *and Devil, you cannot kill me.*

✦ ✦ ✦

The doctors have decided to put Mike into a medically induced coma.

"It is too hard for him to breathe, and we feel that the best thing we can do to help him is to give his mind a rest while his body does its natural healing job. He won't be fighting the machine anymore, and he won't be in pain."

We've agreed to let them do that, after praying together about it first. It's so different now to be in the room with him and not have him "with" us. He's always been the one to keep the communication lines open.

Paulette, Mike's older sister, has decided to stay for as long as he is in the ICU. Her husband, Mel, will stay on for a while. He joins with us in prayer for Mike, as well as for the family members of others we meet in the waiting rooms. Paulette sits with me in the waiting room while Shaun sits with his dad. She's always been the practical one, just like her brother.

"I've been watching the monitors in his room, Sheri, and for a while I felt myself getting really scared for Mike, but then I felt the Lord telling me, 'Yes, you can read the numbers so that you know what to pray about, but don't worry about the numbers, because Mike has been healed.'"

It's not that my mind has been going crazy trying to convince myself that Mike will be okay. I feel the presence of my Father constantly in this room and in Mike's room, but the peace that fills my insides when I hear it from someone else has no match.

Paulette continues: "So I've decided on my action plan. I'm going to put the whole armor of God on Mike every day, as well as pray healing Scriptures over him, especially Psalm 118: 17-18, 'I shall not die, but live, and declare the works of the Lord. The Lord … has not given me over to death.' Mike has always declared the works of the Lord, and he will again."

My spirit is stilled, protected from floating out into currents too strong for it. I can stop here and hang on to catch my breath for a bit before I head back to shore.

✦ ✦ ✦

God has a habit of doing that. Even on our honeymoon we were drifting out to sea. The bed in our Colorado cabin was clean enough; our car, not so much. Writing and toilet paper were still sprawled out in sunbathing mode across the back seat, but hey, it was our honeymoon and we were in the mood for love … and our next LSD hit.

I started to shiver and ambled to the fireplace to get a fire going, but instead of matches, all I could find was a trifold brochure with a picture of Jesus on the front.

Who is on the throne of your life? Is it you or Jesus Christ?

My heartbeat thumped through my chest wall. I knew the answer. I knew the life I was living. I put the trifold back on the mantelpiece and rubbed my arms, now shivering both inside and outside.

Where were those matches?

✦ ✦ ✦

And it's not just Mike's sisters pulling me forward. Sarah, our daughter, has been with us as a tower of faith. I see no fear, in her even though she is fully aware of everything going on.

"It's not that this isn't the worst thing that's ever happened, Mom; it's that I'm not going to focus on how or why. We've asked God to intervene. We believe in his grace. He wants us healthy and healed." She resettles her pregnant body into the hospital chair.

"I want to help Dad myself, and my baby growing inside me, but I'm not the only one who's going to make his recovery happen. We have so much support all around us. I could get really stressed out if I let fear take over, so I'm not going to. The truth is what will help me and you, and it will keep us going strong through all of this. The truth is that this is not what God wanted for Dad. God wants him to have a full recovery."

She rubs her belly and smiles. "God wants him to enjoy his grandkids and pass on everything that's amazing about him."

JANUARY 1, NEW YEAR'S DAY

This doctor keeps looking past my eyes at screens and counters and other people.

"We've given Mike one blood transfusion and he's on the second one now, but we don't know what's happening to the blood. Mike could have organ damage, so we're going to have to run more tests on him to find out where he's bleeding from."

My mind keeps returning to Mike's childhood rattlesnake bite—his hand in the snake hole, the fang in his flesh, the swelling of his skin. His doctor asked for advice because snake bites were not his specialty. He called someone with experience in treating rattlesnake bites, and that call helped save Mike's life. I know I'm thinking about it for more than just history. It's a Holy Spirit nudge, which I follow.

"Is there another doctor you can call to find out where

his blood is going? Who can you call? Is there a doctor here who might know?"

Finally he listens and calls another doctor, who tells him to stop giving the transfusions.

More tests … more lifting him on and off the bed with nine broken ribs, a fractured pelvis, a broken sacrum, a small brain bleed at the base of his head, and extreme pain.

The results are awful. Sally Ann, Mike's other sister, has her hand on my shoulder as we listen.

"Mike has acute renal failure, which means that his kidneys could shut down completely and we'd have to put him on dialysis. The dye that we have to use to perform the CT scan is hard on the kidneys, and that could have contributed to them starting to shut down. This is a very serious condition that Mike might not recover from … the kidneys are supposed to filter all of his body waste and if they stop … worst case scenario … it will cause his body to start shutting down.

"His lung is starting to fill up. We're seeing signs of pneumonia on his X-rays, and the heavy medications we have him on to hold off the pain are not helping his kidneys either. If you are a praying family, I recommend that you do a lot of praying tonight."

We're allowed back into Mike's room. Sally Ann's face says it all, her eyes fixed on the readings on the monitors: BP 98/55, O2 85 percent and dropping…. She's a registered nurse. She knows. I can feel fear trying to trap and suffocate me like a bed pillow. The doctor is fiddling with the ventilator, trying to reset it to bring up Mike's O2 count, and all I can hear are the doctor's words on repeat as I stare at each machine and digital display, each one shouting out, "He's going to die. He's going to die!"

NO! Mike will live and not die. He will live and declare the works of the Lord. I keep repeating this over and over while the doctor and nurse adjust the machines and talk together. The readings keep dropping, dropping to even more dangerous levels. Sally Ann is frozen, her eyes fixed on the numbers. I can almost smell her fear of his impending death.

She will tell me many weeks later that in those moments, she felt he might have only ten minutes left to live, that she became tuned into the sound of the machines and, as she listened, she heard another sound:

The LORD on high is mightier than the noise of many waters, yes, than the mighty waves of the sea (Psalm 93:4).

Despite it all, God's voice was coming through louder and clearer and more powerfully than the noise of many waters, than the breakers of the sea. The "noise of many waters" was used by Satan to try to break her faith and frighten her into weak whispers of prayers.

She takes a deep breath and leaves the room. And all the while Mike lies there in silent helplessness, unaware of what's going on, but I talk to him anyway. Drugs never stopped us from communicating before.

✦ ✦ ✦

And along with the drugs, back in those hazy days, we decided to explore Eastern religions. We started to sit with a spiritual leader, Jeff, and devour his words as if they were jewels of truth

"Don't eat the animals. We have to be kind to the universe and we treat all animals with love.

"Twice a day you need to connect with the universe and let all the thoughts in your head go so you can be one with nature and your fellow man. It's what Buddha wants so that you can be one with him.

"You should come to all our meetings. The more often you come, the more connected you become."

We both wanted desperately to connect with the real thing, the presence that would feed our souls and complete us.

✦ ✦ ✦

Those days are long over. I know I am communicating with my heavenly Father, and I am coming against the powers of the enemy who wants to steal my husband's life.

I touch Mike's cheek with the curve of my fingers, my soft skin against his weathered lines. It's always been that way. He's the tough one, ready to face any storm with courage and resilience. I've hidden behind him, as if behind a windbreaker, and watched him lead well. And now I have a different role. I have to step out into the storm and stand in front. I must let him rest and heal.

I run my finger along his eyebrow to straighten the straggly hairs. I love this face, this man, this ability to be one yet two ,yet two in one.

"Come back to us, Mike. The kids' babies will be here soon. I know how much you are looking forward to that—two little girls ready to change the world with their love. Sarah says you'll be ready to hold her little one by the time she's born. You've given Sarah such an amazing foundation of faith. Thank you for that."

Precious are you ways, O Lord. Thank you in advance for healing him.

OUR WEDDING DAY

6 NO MATTER WHAT

I hold Mike's hand and watch for any signs—a flicker, a twitch of an eyelid, a squeeze of the hand—and wonder if this induced coma is at all similar to his meditative states of old. I hope not. I want nothing to invade his mind that is not straight from heaven, and I pray all the more, until the weight of it all does a belly flop into my soul and I can't hold all the pieces of me together anymore. I leave Mike's room and find a private corner of the ICU. All of the fear and worry and pain whirl out of my eyes. My body shakes and stiffens and collapses. I have no energy left at all. And then Shaun finds me and sits beside me and takes my sniffle-laden hand.

"Mom, everything is going to be okay. Dad is going to make it. This is just a little bump in the road."

He knows how to operate in faith.

I feel surges of life sneak back in to counteract the hopelessness that has invaded my mind and I continue to proclaim, "Mike will live and not die." God's Word truly calms us and brings us peace in our darkest hours.

We stand up. Shaun offers me his arm, walks me to the car, and we drive back to the hotel for the night.

✦ ✦ ✦

And our Eastern spiritual leader back then—the person who offered us his arm, the one we had trusted with our souls—knew there was more too. Jeff took a spiritual retreat in the desert and almost died there in his quest to feel complete, spirit, soul, and body. All of him was so in need of the truth.

But God was watching out for him. He sent people in, where they discovered him and saved his life in more ways than one—they showed him the Scriptures, explained them, and asked him if he wanted to follow the only way, the only truth, the only life.

And he said yes.

He drove back to our house with one of his new friends and together they explained it all over coffee and cookies. I heard the words of truth in that little duplex and I knew. I knew that no matter what Mike ever chose to do in the future, I needed to follow Christ forever. So I did—I came to the Father through Jesus Christ, the only way one can.

✦ ✦ ✦

The children and I are walking down an outdoor path to our hotel room, and to our left is a large tent full of people dressed in finely cut clothes. I hear laughing and applause and see a flash of a white dress that sweeps the floor. Only a few nights ago we were all walking back on this same path together, but now the happiness and the feeling of being present is not with us. My soul is bereft of this loss that has caused me to step into another world of hotel room to waiting room to the ICU.

"He (that's me) will call upon Me, and I will answer him; I will be with him in trouble; I will deliver him and honor him. With a long life I will satisfy him and let him see My salvation" (Psalm 91:15-16 NASB). Mike's assignment on earth is not finished, Lord. Sixty years is not a long life. Mike always said he wanted to be 120 years old. I feel God's strength flooding my spirit again. I will only be moved by God's Word. I will resist the things I see with my eyes. I will not be moved by my emotions. I walk by faith and not by sight.

JANUARY 2

I sit with Mike, pace his room, sit and pace and sit and pace. I talk to him as if he is better. I proclaim Scriptures over him, over the infection the nurses say he has, over his fever. Then my turn is over and I have to let someone else come in.

The day is filled with family and friends who have come to pray with us and bring food and lift our spirits. They all agree with us that Mike's kidneys will work again and that his infection will leave his body. They visit Mike in shifts, and I know that with this much prayer storming the heavens, the devil will have a difficult time trying to make any kind of addition to the bad news of yesterday.

Kanoa, our youth pastor, has brought a video camera, and I let the congregation know about Mike's accident. They suggest planning the service around praying for Mike, and have printed Scriptures to pass out so the prayer can continue during the week. The focus is on what God is doing rather than on the list of things not working in Mike's body right now. I'm 100 percent in agreement.

✦ ✦ ✦

We pray in tongues together—another of the new things we learned from Jeff after his trip from death into life back in '72. We wanted that closer connection to God that words alone could not bring.

"The Holy Spirit gives you power—not the kind of power you feel after taking a hit or doing an hour of meditation, but heaven's power," Jeff said.

"And you get that rush of bravery that helps you talk to other people about Jesus.

"And you're able to pray for people with words you've never learned before."

Jeff's friend, Jock, was excited, and his shiny eyes and willingness to share tantalized us with the power and love of God. We'd thought we were done when we prayed "the prayer," but apparently there was much more! God wanted us to be filled with the Holy Spirit. We wanted it all—everything God had for us—and boy, did we get it!

✦ ✦ ✦

By the time the sun is laying his head behind the wall of daylight, things have turned a little. The nurses don't trudge around the room so sadly. The numbers on the machines are somewhat better. Shaun sits with me.

"Mom, just like Isaiah 46 says, we're 'declaring the end from the beginning, and from ancient times things that are not yet done,' so we're saying that Dad is already whole and healed and better than he was before this accident. We're seeing him through eyes of faith—seeing and believing what God is doing even before we see the proof of it in the natural.

"I really feel like Dad's going to be okay, just like you've been praying all along. He's going to live."

Raising Sarah and Shaun by faith and not fear was always our greatest desire, and now the tears swell again.

"Mom, what's wrong?"

I sniff and try to find a tissue in my purse. "I just always thought that my focus on raising you and Sarah on the promises of God was for you, not me!"

He puts an arm around my shoulders and pulls me closer. The now silent peace of our faith helps me breathe as I dab my nose and fill up on the Holy Spirit again.

We have always been a close family, choosing to do life with our children rather than for them while they were growing up. We always encouraged them to be open about things they were going through so we could push through together, and now they are returning the favor. I sneak a look at them both and thank God for being such a good Father to us over the years, and even today.

✦ ✦ ✦

"Yea, you can even pray in tongues when you're filled with the Holy Spirit!" Jeff told us several times.

Mike glanced sideways to see my reaction, but I'd heard about this tongues business before. I just wasn't sure about how it was going to go down.

A few weeks later, we'd seen it and heard it through the new friends we'd made, and we headed to the church altar to make our desire for all of God public. We will always remember that day, and Ken Hagin Jr's life-changing words.

✦ ✦ ✦

Thank you, Lord, for the gift of tongues. So many times I've been at a loss for how to pray, and you have come through every time with the words and sounds that reach heaven. Thank you for flesh and blood family and spiritual family— for the love and support and meals and practical help they have given us over these last few days.

Thank you for the lifelong friends who have been with us since the early days of our journey into intimacy with you. Thank you for the leaders who walked beside us, mentored us, and taught us how to read your Word and see it come alive before our eyes. Thank you for the Hagins.

Thank you for the couples who invested in our marriage and taught Mike and me how to love and honor each other. Thank you for the commitment they modeled for us that helped us to never even consider divorce and always work through our issues with clear communication.

Thank you, thank you, thank you. You are a good God, and I choose to trust you, no matter what.

I still feel a little shaky, but I don't feel alone. The Holy Spirit hovers and rests within. We have made it through another day.

Santa Fe is so familiar to my senses, and tonight is no exception. I follow the curves of her narrow streets and breathe her in. I grew up here, filling my youth and curiosity with her art galleries and museums. Friends' homes always had a Native American blanket or two, and turquoise jewelry was a given. Beauty thrives here in the talented hands of masters.

The city snuggles into the crook of an army of mountains, and even though it's pitch black outside, I can hear the swish of Mike's skis on the silver snow of the Sangre de Cristo Mountains. I feel his pleasure. One day we will come back to celebrate God's gift of life.

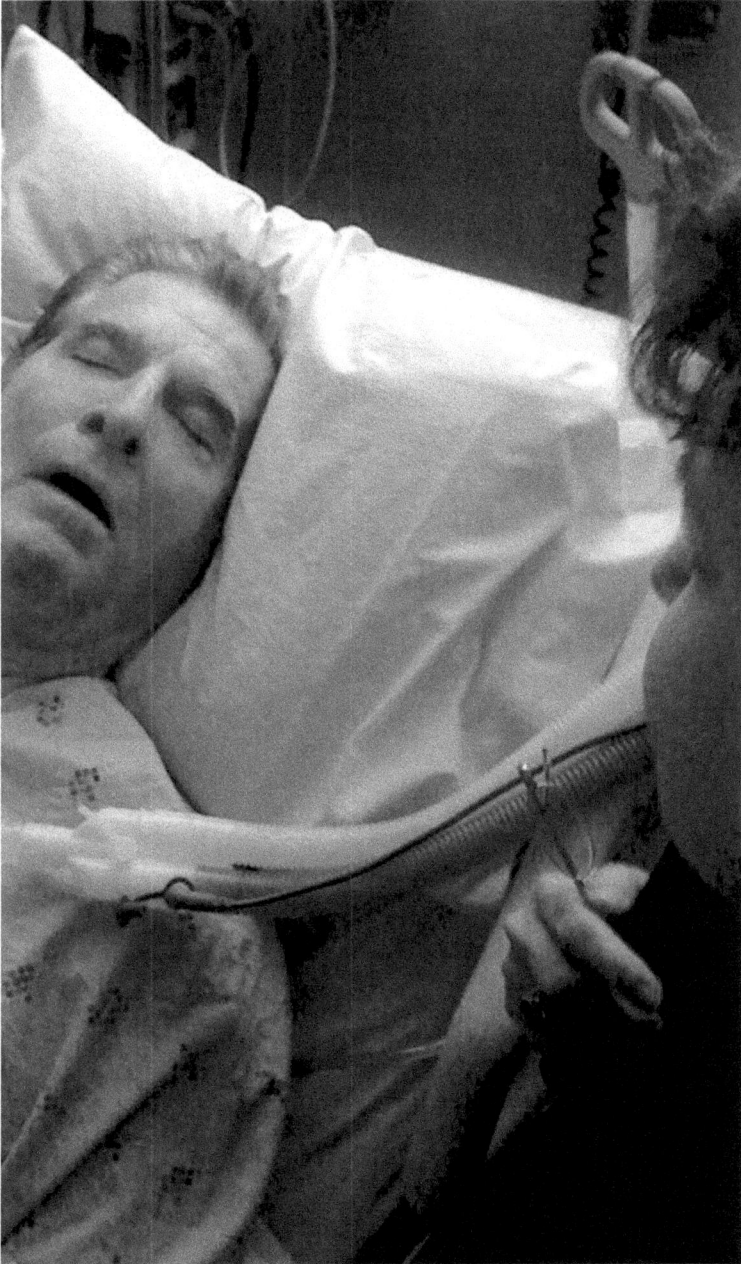

THE EVER-FAITHFUL PAULETTE

7

THE PRESENCE OF OTHERS

JANUARY 3

It's Sunday morning and I'm in Santa Fe driving to the hospital instead of to church. A Sunday without church has always left me feeling out of sorts. It marks the week for me, reminds me of the goodness of God, helps me to stay connected to those I love, and realigns me for the week ahead.

I can picture it all happening in my head—the worship with hands in the air and knees on the floor; the huddles of couples and families and friends around the room as they share communion; the reflections and revelation shared from the pulpit. It's where we belong.

✦ ✦ ✦

Peace, not war! We were smack dab in the center of the hippie movement, and so many of us flooded local churches in our quest for truth. We had a knack for disturbing congregations stuck in the way things "should be." We were Jesus freaks, and the only way we knew things should be was Jesus's way. Our hearts beat to do his will, and we didn't care about long hair and bare feet. We were ready to worship to beats that reflected the music of our generation.

We spent almost every night at our little church, devouring Scripture and renewing our minds with it. My gratefulness to our mentors in how to "do life together" goes beyond words.

✦ ✦ ✦

Mike's condition hasn't changed much over the last two days. Family members are talking about leaving and heading back to their respective jobs. Thankfully, I will not be alone here. Mike's sisters have decided to stay for a few more days; and Shaun, Sarah, and Jason will be back next weekend.

A hospital security worker enters the waiting room while the travel plans continue.

"Is anyone here the owner of a white Yukon?"

"Sheri, that's you!" Jason walks over to the man, chats for a moment, and sits back down beside me. "You must have parked sideways this morning! Got the keys?"

I realize again that I am still traveling in and out of this otherworld. I struggle to remember where I parked the SUV, and I have no idea how I managed to park it diagonally across the parking spaces. Maybe I can blame it on the snow.... .

"It's okay, Mom. This man is going to show me where it is."

I've forgotten what normal feels like.

It's Monday morning and I'm trying to put this new life together and make it as normal as possible. My first call is to Doug Jones, the alumni director from our days at Rhema Bible Training Center (now Rhema Bible College). He's given us sound advice during other difficult times in our lives, and his wisdom is what I need right now.

"You know, Sheri," Doug says, "you might not want to list off every tiny detail of what's wrong with Mike, but faith doesn't deny the facts. Don't be afraid of telling your church family everything, because we know the truth of God's Word will change the facts. Go ahead and let your congregation know everything that's going on, but let them know your stance so that you are all on the same page and praying *from* a place of victory instead of *into* a place of victory."

The pen is still in my hand, poised over the pristine sheet of paper I am ready to write my checklist on, and Doug's words speak to my heart and stay there. There is no checklist for the heart. I know he is ever the practical one, though, so I am ready for the plan—a way forward that will give me something beneficial to do to help our church family project its faith with mine.

"So who do you tell first when you get updates from the doctors?"

"Um, usually whoever is in the room with me or calls me next on the phone."

"That's not a good idea, and here's why: You need to tell your family first, so Sarah, Shaun, and other family members need to be first in line for that kind of news. Then call Becky so she can send out news to the church. She can be your key information person there. Once you've given family and Becky the latest information, then record a new voicemail on your phone so that it can automatically respond to people who are not in your inner circle. That way they will still get updated news for their prayer times, and you can spend more quality time with Mike and the family."

Sarah and Shaun

In-laws

Becky

Voicemail

Facts vs. truth of God's Word and Scriptures

"Another thing, Sheri: make sure you are never alone. The devil sure takes advantage of us when we're in situations like this, and it's just not good to be by yourself."

I flash back to that time in the corner of ICU with Shaun beside me. Doug is right—I need the presence of others.

Never alone

My next call is to Becky, one of our most trusted pastors.

"Sheri, yesterday's service was amazing. So many people came up afterward and asked to sign up for a shift on the 24-hour prayer roster for Mike and the family. People want to take on more responsibility for you. The feeling of unity here has grown overnight."

"That's so good to hear. I talked to Doug Jones today, and he suggested I come and talk to the congregation next Sunday—he said that way I can help the congregation stay hooked in faith with me. I'm going to come and do that."

"And that's all we'd like from you. Don't worry about

anything else. We've got it all covered."

Becky has always been so reliable and steady—a true godsend.

Share next Sunday

JANUARY 6

One of Mike's doctors is waiting for me when I walk into the ICU.

"Mrs. Schaefer, we need to do a tracheotomy and insert a feeding tube into your husband's stomach. Being intubated is like having a straw stuck in your throat, and we would like to make it even easier on your husband and have his airflow go through the trach tube instead. We will make an incision at the base of his throat and connect a tube from there to the breathing machine."

I feel relief about the tracheotomy. Mike has been intubated for too long, and I want him to be as comfortable as possible. I am also glad that he will be receiving nourishment through a feeding tube.

I step into his room and watch him lying there, wishing I could wake up beside him in the mornings and sit with him over breakfast. I miss our conversations. I miss the surety of everyday life, his smiles, his phone calls asking me to get milk on the way home, the way he holds my hand. When he gets out of this place, I don't want to take those moments for granted ever again.

✦ ✦ ✦

I never imagined, back in those carefree college years, that Mike would one day be a pastor and I'd be the pastor's wife. We prayed and believed for a boy and a girl, and we were blessed with Sarah and Shaun. We moved into the comfortable life, which I loved, until Mike sat with me and broke the news that he felt that he was supposed to go to Rhema Bible Training Center in Broken Arrow, Oklahoma. Where the heck was that?

I argued with God for months. Moving would upset everything and require us to have to start over in every way. And then, to top it off, God used Dean Moffatt to speak to me about attending the college as well,. Smack dab in the middle of Mike's interview, he said,

"And will you be coming too?"

"To be honest, I hadn't really thought about that being a possibility."

"Can you imagine Mike coming home from school each day and trying to tell you about everything he learned? We find that when couples attend together and share the experience, their marriages grow."

✦ ✦ ✦

I can now look back and see the wisdom of the Lord. I really believe that our going to Bible school was more for me than him. Mike and I were living separate lives—he in his business and I with our children—and it would take something that drastic to shake us up and throw us back toward each other. God would give us a plan for our lives that would be bigger than ourselves.

The thought that I might lose him now ....

I keep going back over the morning of the accident. I remember Mike sitting back in his chair after that huge breakfast, saying that he really didn't want to ski that day. I recall thinking, *Man, after all we ate, I wouldn't want to ski either.* What I probably said was, "Oh, once you get rolling you'll be fine."

I wonder what would have happened if I'd paid more attention, if I'd asked God about it, if I'd been more in the Spirit. Could I have stopped all of this from happening? Was Mike's feeling more of a warning from the Holy Spirit? Shaun even told his dad that he didn't have to ski that second day because David was coming up to join them.

I had skied all during high school at the Santa Fe Ski Basin with friends without an accident. I suppose it never crossed my mind because neither I nor my friends had ever experienced one. But should I have known?

In my soul I know that what-ifs are never a good idea, but *what if …?* But then I stop myself. The past has passed, and my responsibility is to focus on the *now*. God has not given me a spirit of fear, but of power and of love and of a sound mind. God is with me. He is amazing grace. My job is to walk with him.

8

FAMILY

JANUARY 8

Mike's fever seems to be the same as it has been every other day—up and down—but it gets very high at night. The doctors say they are satisfied with his condition today.

I look at Mike every day in this hospital bed, a man with his soul on silent, at least to those around him. Our new routine brings its own strange comfort. Every day strangers wash him and turn him, straighten his covers, check his vitals, and leave. Because of a viral outbreak, we are only allowed in to see him twice a day—two hours in the morning and two at night.

We all have rooms on the same floor at the hotel. Sally Ann or my two children are in the room next to mine, and Paulette is a few doors down. We have fit into a new routine, these familial intercessors and I. Every morning we get up and pray. I usually call the night nurse before she leaves to see what kind of night Mike has had. We eat in the room or go down to breakfast. We get in a little time on the treadmill, make calls, change the message on my phone (if needed), and work on e-mails. At about 11:15 or so we head to the hospital.

Many days church members bring up food and visit and pray with us from 12 to 2 p.m. We usually only let family members in to see Mike, for two reasons: It can be very upsetting to them, and the hospital suggested that we do so. On the weekends, family and friends from church fill up the waiting room and it looks like we have taken it over. It's a transition, one I was definitely unprepared for, but I am so thankful to see everyone and pray with them.

During the week we are in a smaller waiting room, and when other patients' visitors come in, we ask them about their stories and end up praying for their loved ones in ICU. We feel like we are in the foxhole with them each day, hiding out and taking turns at firing upon enemy lines. I don't think anyone has declined our requests to pray for him or her, and we see the Spirit bring measures of peace, healing, and gratitude to many hearts.

✦ ✦ ✦

Our shift into student life at Rhema began well. Mike and I were able to share our love for the Lord with each other again, and many were the nights we spent discussing the latest lesson and what it meant for us as a couple and as parents. Kenneth E. Hagin's teachings on faith, walking in love, forgiveness, healing, and having our home in order changed the focus of our lives. Together, we decided to always place God and our family before ministry.

✦ ✦ ✦

I think that's one of the many reasons why I don't feel alone here in the hospital. Two things that bring me comfort are the presence of God and family. We are still doing life together.

Today Mel, my brother-in-law, needs swimming trunks, so we stop at the Wal-Mart on the way back to the hotel. I feel like I've been here before, but in a dream. Clothing racks glare, people don't look the same as the familiar family members in our waiting room, the woman at the checkout doesn't feel like a real person. A few weeks before the accident, everything would have seemed normal about this simple task. Not now. My new "normal" does not include a trip to Wal-Mart.

JANUARY 10

I'm back in Albuquerque to see my church family! Even as my feet cross the threshold, the sounds of conversations and laughter fill my ears and warm my heart. The presence of God in these people, in this place, surrounds me and lifts me heavenward.

I've had a lot of time to prepare for this morning, and I'm ready to share. In a way, I am grateful that the years of teaching from Bible college classes and former pastors are bearing fruit. The Word is never meant to help us merely acquire knowledge, but to bring life to people that are struggling and losing their grip.

I look out into the faces Mike and I have loved over the years. So many representations of the love of God in one place, and we get to be the ones to do life with them. It's been both an honor and a privilege.

Addressing the congregation, I begin by saying, "I want to share with you a portion of Acts 4:24, the part where Peter and John reported all that the chief priests and elders had said to them. I am here to report the *all* of Pastor Mikes accident to you."

I go over the details of Mike's ski accident and the subsequent medical care he has received for those parts of his body that have not yet healed. And then I lay it out—the reason for our faith:

"As many of you are aware, Mike has nine broken ribs and a distressed left lung, because the fractured ribs were unable to hold his lung in place. He has a fractured pelvis, a broken sacrum, and a small brain bleed in the back of his head from hitting the ground after hitting the tree. Mike was intubated and on a ventilator, and he has since been given a temporary tracheostomy tube to help him breathe more easily.

"As believers in the body of Jesus Christ, we know that when Jesus was crucified on the cross, his blood was shed for our sins to be forgiven. I didn't know for a number of years that Jesus not only died for our sins, he also provided physical healing for us—by the stripes on his back caused by the beating he took.

"As I read the book *Christ the Healer* by F.F. Bosworth, I began to get the revelation that is recorded in 1 Peter 2:24. The Amplified Bible reads, 'He personally bore our sins in his [own] body on the tree [as on an altar and offered Himself on it], that we might die [cease to exist] to sin and live to righteousness. By his wounds you have been healed.'

"I noticed 'have been' in this passage is past tense. We know from Romans 10:17 that faith comes by hearing the Word of God. For years now, I have spent time daily in God's Word to find his will. I believe my faith has grown because of that.

"Charles Capps, in his book *God's Creative Power* says,

> *Faith is in two places. It is in our hearts (mind and spirit) and in our mouths. Romans 10:8 asks, "But what does it say? The Word (God's message in Christ) is near you, on your lips and in your heart; that is, the Word (the message, the basis and object) of faith which we preach" (Deut. 30:14 AMP). We release our faith through speaking what God's Word says about any given situation. To put it another way, faith is simply taking God's Word for granted.*

"Dr. Myles Munroe, in his book *Understanding the Purpose and Power of Prayer*, says,

> *The Word of God says so much about faith. Romans 1:17 says that the just shall live by faith. Hebrews 11:6 tells us that without faith it is impossible to please God. The New Testament word "faith" comes from the Greek word pistis, which means belief or confidence. Having faith means believing and having confidence in the words that you hear or read.*

"And in his book *Bible Prayer Study Course*, Kenneth E. Hagin says,

> *You must see yourself in possession of what you've asked for and make plans accordingly as if it were already a reality.*

"Mike and I have operated on these truths for many years and have seen so many things come to pass that we believed for, both in our personal lives and in the lives of all of you here at Church Alive!

"There are so many misconceptions regarding what faith is or what it isn't. One thing faith is not is denying the facts. Some people think denying the facts will cause them to go away. No; however, the truth of God's Word can change the facts as we believe them and then declare and decree them from our mouths. There is power in believing and speaking God's Word into the everyday situations we face. Charles Capps says in his book *God's Creative Power,* 'The word of God conceived in the heart, formed by the tongue, and spoken out of the mouth is creative power.'

"Isaiah 46:10 in the Amplified Bible says, 'Declaring the end and the result from the beginning….' I know from Proverbs 12:21 that the power of life and death is in the tongue. At the beginning of this whole misadventure, I sensed what I needed to do was first to believe, which I did. Then I was to proclaim, by faith in God's Word and his will, the outcome of how everything would end up *before* I actually saw it come to pass in the natural. I would speak faith that Mike would live and not die and 'declare the works and recount the illustrious acts of the Lord' (Psalm 118:17 AMP).

"According to I Peter 2:24, by Jesus's stripes, Mike is whole and healed and in better health than before the accident. Please be in agreement with me to believe and to say the same things I am believing and saying. We are not going to talk among ourselves about the negative things that are going on—the problems or complications—but we will all come together and decree and declare, before we see it with our eyes, what God had already accomplished and done for us on the cross and has said in his Word.

"Psalm 119:89 tells us, 'Forever, O Lord, Your word is settled in heaven.' What God has said in his Word is already established in heaven. We will see it come to pass as we declare it on the earth. Romans 4:17 refers to God who gives life to the dead and speaks of the nonexistent things that he has foretold and promised as if they already existed. As a body of believers, we are going to believe in our hearts the Scriptures that God has promised us about healing. We were going to say by faith that Pastor Mike is healed and whole before we actually see it with our eyes. The nonexistent thing at this point in time is Pastor Mike's healing, but we are seeing his body whole and healed in the spiritual realm before we see it in the natural realm.

"Charles Capps, in *God's Creative Power for Healing,* says this is not such a far out concept.

> *This is is a SPIRITUAL LAW. God never does anything without saying it first. God is a faith God. God released His faith in Words. "And Jesus answering saith unto them, Have faith in God" (Mark 11:22). A more literal translation of the above verse says "Have the God kind of faith, or faith of God." Ephesians 5:1 literally tells us to be imitators of God as children imitate their parents. To imitate God, you must talk like Him and act like Him. He would not ask you to do something you are not capable of doing.*

"So here's the battle plan: Let's all hook up together in faith and believe that our pastor will live and not die. You should all have received a two-page handout containing the specific Scriptures to pray every day. I will keep you informed by e-mail every two to three days as to Mike's progress. I will also share the specific things we need to target weekly and day-by-day in prayer."

The family of God mills about after the service, hugging me, agreeing with me in faith, encouraging me. These people have my heart. Their love and support boost my resolve, and I know we can get through this together. With resolve, family, and the Holy Spirit, I can do anything.

But now Mike has to go through more intervention.

MIKE PRAYING OVER HIS GRANDDAUGHTER

9 A DIFFICULT PROCEDURE

Yet again, the doctors have to do a surgical procedure. This one involves putting a screw into Mike's fractured sacrum to make sure it heals the right way. While he could heal without it, having the screw in place can help reduce neurological damage once he gets up and about. Ahh, that sounds so good—I am looking forward to the day when Mike can function fully again.

We head to downtown Santa Fe to eat while the surgery is in progress—something we have done from time to time when a day goes by without someone bringing food. We never go hungry. The family of God is good at many things when it comes to comfort, and I think one of its best gifts is in the provision of meals when life is disrupted by accidents, new babies, or death.

The snow is aplenty today, as it is every day, bringing freshness with each new snowfall. I was raised in Santa Fe until I graduated from high school, and I never tire of its history and artistry. We drive past downtown's ever busy plaza. Native Americans sell blankets and turquoise jewelry in front of the Palace of the Governors, while the jewelry, clothing, and bronze sculptures of many nations beckon through the storefronts.

We also pass the Loretto Chapel, one of my favorite attractions because of its miraculous staircase that was built without nails. It is said that a carpenter showed up one night and told the nuns at the chapel that he would build the staircase so badly needed for the choir to get up to the loft. When the magnificent curved structure was finished, the carpenter disappeared without a word or compensation. Some feel he was an angel. It wouldn't surprise me. God has sent us many angels through our lives to help us ascend in faith and circumstances.

Unfortunately Mike's rise to full health is not without some delays; however, we receive word that the doctors are pleased with the success of the surgery. We are one day closer to Mike coming home.

JANUARY 14

"Mrs. Schaefer, we've done a CT scan and discovered some blood clots in your husband's heart and lungs. The one in his lung is very large, and it's causing his heart to race. We're going to give him Coumadin, a blood thinner, but we'll need to keep a close eye on him in case we need to take further action."

We pray a lot today, and have updated the church prayer line with the information, but sadly the news is not good by evening. The medical team agrees it needs to filter the clots so his blood can continue to flow properly.

"To do this, we have to insert a filter into a large vein in his abdomen to trap large clot fragments and stop them from reaching his brain, heart, or lungs, which could be fatal. We first insert a catheter into the vein and then insert the filter through the catheter. Once it's in the right position, we release the filter so that it can expand and attach itself to the blood vessel's walls.

"However, there is a serious risk of his body reacting badly to this procedure because of his poor kidney function and his previous brain bleed. The blood vessel might be damaged, bruised, or even burst at the puncture site. The IVC filter might change position and penetrate the vein.

"We also need to break up the clot close to his heart, and we can do that by inserting another catheter and pointing it directly at the blood clot before releasing clot-dissolving enzymes.

"As far as we see it, the preemptive filter for his blood clots today could save his life, but we need your permission to go ahead with it."

I do not feel at all comfortable about the risks associated with filtering his blood clots. I've been close to losing this man many times over in the last two weeks, and this new procedure is difficult to take in. Every day I've been declaring Mike's healing, and these men want to do something which could introduce more infection and take Mike's life. Do the benefits outweigh the risk? My decision could change everything.

Shaun has become my right-hand man of God. I look at him and see his years of bugs, snakes, sports, and adventure-loving ways. I now get to be the recipient of his openness and ministry experience. Such a circle God weaves! Sarah, with her ability to size up a situation and organize it into doable steps, brings clarity to my days. She has no fear. Her faith sometimes surpasses mine. Having Mike's sisters here, with all of their medical experience, is invaluable. I have to make the decision quickly, and I am so relieved I am not alone. In the end, we decide that the dangers of not doing the procedure are higher than the risks of doing it. We pray until we feel the peace of God that bypasses our minds and all of the medical jargon. Yes, they can do it.

They begin at 11 p.m.

JANUARY 16

It's been over twenty-four hours, and it looks like the procedure was successful, praise God! And to add to the good news, today the respiratory therapist will start weaning Mike off the ventilator!

"Your husband's vitals are good. His pain seems to be managed well, and he is healing well from all of his surgeries. We've been slowly reducing his oxygen levels, his lungs are still improving, and his blood count looks good, so today we can see just how well he can breathe on his own."

She turns to Mike. "It might hurt a bit to use muscles you haven't had to use in quite a while. We'll be watching everything the whole time to make sure you're doing well, so there's no need to worry about not being able to breathe."

Mike is ready to make it happen, and we wait outside while they sit him upright in a chair.

I sit with him again and hold his hand as he begins to break free from this machine that has helped him so much over the last weeks. The thought of him being one step closer to full healing is dizzying. God is so good.

Our family is so good. Our church family is so good. The power of prayer has held us all up and brought us to this point. He has captured all our prayers and poured the answers back over us, and I can feel his presence in this room while Mike breathes in and out, in and out with very little help from the ventilator. My soul exalts the Lord, and my spirit has rejoiced in God my Savior.

Mike continues to breathe mostly on his own for three hours. The therapist connects him back up for the rest of the day, but today was a big day and Mike has passed with flying colors.

✦   ✦   ✦

God knows how much I needed to develop my faith, and I am so grateful for the anchor I have in the Rock that holds me close. I mostly talked through my Sunday School years of instruction, but I listened at Rhema BTC. Kenneth E. Hagin's passion for faith and its application through the Holy Spirit was mesmerizing and infective. We soaked up stories and insights about the character and heart of God in the mornings and then had to immediately enact the lessons once we left the campus. Our hearts were transformed because we didn't just learn about God; we learned how to become more like him by being with him.

The embers of our marriage were fanned and nurtured until Mike and I were thinking and praying and listening to each other in a way we hadn't for years. He became my best friend again. We liked and respected each other. We could see our hearts again.

Rev. Doug Jones, the director of the Rhema Alumni Association, also became our friend over those years. One of our favorite teachers, he spearheaded my revelation of healing—that Jesus took it all on his own body so I could be completely free from all sin and sickness.

✦ ✦ ✦

Doug and Pastor Ken Hagin have been praying for us and communicating since the day of the accident, yet again being the hands and feet of the Jesus they preach. I know in my heart and spirit that it is God's will for Mike to be healed and that he was healed the first time we prayed, according to the Word of God. This is the truth of God's Word whether I can, right now, see that healing in Mike's body or not. We have an anchor that keeps the soul *steadfast and sure as the billows roll, fastened to the rock which cannot move, grounded firm and deep in the Savior's love!*

A phone call confirms God's faithfulness: It's the regional manager of the hotel we're staying in.

"Mrs. Schaefer, the hotel chain has decided to cover the room charge for the length of your stay here, given the extent of your husband's injuries and everything you are going through right now." He pauses. "How is he doing today?"

I'm swallowing and swimming for the right words to say, but I can't find them. Relief surges up to my eyes and I feel small yet empowered. God, thank you that you will work out and cover all the expenses for us, in Jesus's name.

✦ ✦ ✦

We are no strangers to God's miraculous provision. I dragged my feet out of our beautiful home and income bracket, only feeling okay about going because I had put out a "fleece" and told God I would attend Bible school if certain conditions were met. I thought he would see things my way.

First, I asked God to sell the apartments we owned so we

could have money to live on until Mike got a part-time job.

Secondly, I wanted to live in a neighborhood where there were children to play with my kids.

And lastly, I desired to use the money from our retirement account.

I was asking that we wouldn't have to live by faith at all, that everything would be quite comfortable. My distaste for poverty gave God the last laugh. He was so much bigger! I thought God had answered all my demands when we had an offer on the apartments;. We found a duplex on a street where there were kids our children's ages, and we got the money I wanted from our retirement account. Things appeared perfect … but then the deal on the apartments fell through, Mike had difficulty finding a part-time job, and we went through the retirement money pretty quickly. It was because of that time of reliance on God's promises that our faith in his provision grew. It would lay the foundation for our faith levels in our future.

After Bible school, we started over financially yet again. Ten years after that, we started a new church and left behind another secure lifestyle. Once again we had an opportunity to trust God to provide for us. Now, however, our mortgage payment was no longer $95 a month, and we had two children in high school with college in their futures. I remember that Brother Hagin said—in one of his courses on faith and finances—"When you obey God, payday always comes." He said that we would probably have many opportunities to trust God in this area. He was right!

✦ ✦ ✦

And now it's morning again, and I look at Mike and know that serving the Lord with my husband has always been an adventure, and not just when it comes to finances, thanks to Mike's bold and daring spirit. He's the risk taker, the one to paddle the boat upstream in the rapids while I stand on the banks and beg him to come float on a raft in calmer waters. Being married to him has stretched me like a rubber band at times, but God has been so very faithful and payday always comes.

My thoughts move to the many group trips we took into China as Bible smugglers. Mike, as always, led the way, and we were able to place God's precious words of life into the hands of fellow brothers and sisters in Christ. To imagine daily life without God's Word is impossible. We were willing to take that risk time and time again because of it.

I squeeze his hand. "I wouldn't change following God's will for anything."

We share a knowing smile. There is so much to do to expand God's kingdom on earth and take the message of his great love to others. I am so privileged to be one piece of the plan.

But sometimes things don't go according to plan ....

ONE OF MIKE'S ADVENTURES

10

HOPE DEFERRED

JANUARY 18

The doctor's smile stretches widely across his thin face. "Mrs. Schaefer, we're very pleased with your husband's progress, so much so that we are talking about moving him to another facility that specializes in helping people get off the trach tube. There's a respiratory hospital in Albuquerque that should have a bed available tomorrow."

GOD IS SO GOOD! Bless the Lord, oh my soul, and all that is within me, bless his holy name!

I run back to Mike and kiss his face and cup it in my hands. "They're moving you! To another hospital where you can get this thing out of your neck! You'll be able to talk again, and we can go home soon!" I can hear myself jabbering, but I don't care. Mike's grinning the whole time, and my feet are so light I'm almost dancing.

JANUARY 19

I've set the alarm for an early morning leap out of bed. Today is the day, the day things change for the better. This is the day!

And then one phone call changes everything. Again.

This same doctor who promised me the moon yesterday now says there is no bed available in the other hospital today, and that Mike has a fever anyway … that it wouldn't be smart to move him because he doesn't know what's causing the fever and he'd rather find the source and treat it before a move.

Deep in my soul I know he's right, that it's all about what's best for Mike. But it's like the hot air balloon was full and then a storm blew in and I'm still sitting on the ground in a straw basket with no sign of liftoff, not to mention the downpour.

I can't.

I just can't.

But I know I can. I have to.

But I stay in bed most of the day anyway. Hope deferred makes the heart sick, so I'm taking a self-appointed sick day to hang out with the Father and regroup in time for the evening visit.

JANUARY 20

I'm looking very deliberately for the good, the positive, the God-at-work moments, and today Mike is able to move his arms more. It's a little thing, but it's a big deal at the same time because God is in it.

✦ ✦ ✦

It brings me back to a Sunday morning when we were holding services at a hotel. Mike had left his sermon notes at home, so I sped back to get them. I got to the house, only to realize I didn't have a house key on the ring of keys he gave me. I knew I had only twenty minutes before Mike was to start preaching, so the Holy Spirit and I started to strategize. We had an upstairs bedroom with an outside balcony, whose door we rarely locked. I grabbed a ladder from the side of the house and laid it up to the top of the balcony wall, but I knew I would need a supernatural boost as well as incredible arm strength to pull myself up to the top and over that wall. *Holy Spirit, you know how much I need you now. I can't do this on my own—only you can make it happen.*

The next moment I was at the top of the wall and into the house, and then back at the hotel just as praise and worship was ending. Now here is the real kicker: I knew I had supernatural intervention from the Lord, because I did all that and didn't even get a run in my nylons!

✦ ✦ ✦

JANUARY 22

I go into Mike's room today to see him hooked up to IV antibiotics. The doctor found the cause of his fever—a blood infection which should start to clear up in the next twenty-four hours.

Mike is in good spirits today. He's even started a little physical therapy.

JANUARY 25

I really truly thought I'd be visiting Mike in a different facility by now, yet here we are. I wish time travel were real and we could fast-forward a few months. We'd be sitting at our kitchen table, checking e-mails and sipping our morning coffee, the comfortable silence settling around us like a light flurry of snow. Mike would lift his head and before the first word, I'd speak his sentence.

He's always been the strong one, the one to look after us all, to be there when we need anything at all. His name means "who is like God," and he truly is. To now be so weak and helpless bothers him a lot, and today made that even worse for him. He pulled out his trach tube by mistake and it had to be reinserted. The nurses didn't trust him to not pull it out again, and now he's lying here with his hands restrained for the rest of the night.

✦ ✦ ✦

It reminds me of the time I suffered from my own childhood "accident." My stomach had started to ache so badly that I was admitted for overnight observation. Halfway through the darkest hours, I jumped into full waking mode when I realized that my pain was my own doing—I had sneaked into a neighbor's yard that afternoon and helped myself to a large number of his green apples. Naturally, I didn't volunteer said information to my parents, and I certainly didn't have my hands restrained over it, although my guilt and fear of discovery were far greater than any spanking they might have imposed.

✦ ✦ ✦

I stroke Mike's hair again. He still hasn't been given the release to go to Albuquerque. *Thank you, Father, that if we don't quit we win! We continue to thank you, Lord, for clear lungs for Mike.*

JANUARY 26

Today is the day! Today is the day Mike is being transferred to Albuquerque.

I check out of the hotel, so grateful to the people at the front desk and everyone who made our stay so nice, and head home. Home!

And I walk into our home to find it completely spotless! All the Christmas decorations are boxed and packed away; the garage is clean; the house has been scrubbed and dusted and vacuumed by our church family. Blessing upon blessing has fed my soul and spirit on an already glorious day.

The drive to the hospital is quick, and my hot air balloon has finally lifted into the blue sky with no more downpours in the forecast. Kindred Hospital is a respiratory facility that specializes in helping people get off a tracheostomy tube. They are very good at what they do, but Mike will no longer be in an ICU unit. He'll be in a room with one nurse to seven patients. It makes me a bit edgy knowing that he won't have the same level of surveillance he has had up to this point in his recovery, but God is good and his angels are constantly watching over Mike.

After thirty-two days in Santa Fe, I climb into my own bed and rest my head on my own pillow. I know that tonight I will sleep well.

JANUARY 30

Only four days have passed, yet so much has happened so quickly! Mike's medication was slowly reduced, so he is much more alert and able to communicate a bit more. He has been getting daily physical therapy and speech therapy. He's able to stand for a few minutes at a time, and the nurses are helping me to support him in more practical ways with his recovery.

It is still very difficult to understand Mike, but we are getting better at figuring out what he wants. His speech is still very slurred and his tongue is not functioning well. The doctor says the left side of the tongue has atrophied, which is probably due to the brain bleed, but he expects him to recover the use of it.

We can now sit Mike in the wheelchair and park him in a spot where he can look out the window into the hospital garden. He's lost a lot of weight and is still on the feeding tube, so we are praying for a quick recovery for that. He had always looked healthy, and this skinny model look doesn't suit him at all.

Our prayer focus has changed from the urgent to the ongoing healing journey Mike is on. This week it is for clear lungs, for his trach to be out, and for supernatural strength. I thought we were in the clear, but I didn't know there was one more obstacle Satan would try to throw our way, despite his being on the losing team from day one….

ON THE MEND

11

YOU KNOW

FEBRUARY 5

It's been another five days of hard work on Mike's part, and today they have removed his tracheostomy tube! They will keep him on the feeding tube, and if he passes a swallow test, he might be able to handle some thickened liquids. Thank you, Jesus!

FEBRUARY 8

Mike was released today from Kindred Hospital. He is now at another facility for rehab. He will receive physical therapy, speech therapy, and occupational therapy. His journey back to full health continues.

If I'm completely honest, I look back and am astounded at how God has come through in so many ways. In each of the trying moments, in the times when I could have doubted God, in times when our hopes were crushed, God came through. No matter what happened, he was with me; his heart was mine; my heart was his. And at the end of it all, that's what matters. He is my peace.

FEBRUARY 9

It's about 5:30 in the morning and the phone rings, jolting me to a blur of semi-consciousness.

"Sheri, it's me. I'm so sorry for calling you so early, but I'm in so much pain. It's in my left thigh area."

It's unusual for Mike to complain of pain, and on top of that, to wake me at such an early hour, but I'm not fully awake or thinking along these lines.

"Have you talked to the doctor? Oh, he's only on call? Well, call him, because it sounds really bad. I'll get dressed and come in as soon as I can."

I walk into the hospital room to find that the doctor has already seen Mike.

"He says it's just a charley horse. I got a muscle relaxer, but I can't handle this pain."

I can feel my anger bubbling up from the murky depths of my soul. *So many times, Lord, so many times throughout this ordeal, we get through one hurdle and then something else happens. When are we going to get a break?* But then I start talking to my soul, just like David did.

Emotions, get in line. Negative thoughts, you will leave. This mental and emotional space is not for rent. Word of God, come and fill me up. It's by faith and patience I inherit the promises of healing for Mike. Holy Spirit, fill me with faith and patience so I can stay steady and strong in you.

I have to keep repeating this prayer for the next forty-eight hours, because his pain never lessens.

FEBRUARY 11

One of the nurses insisted that Mike be taken by ambulance to another hospital to have doctors determine the cause of the pain, and … it turns out Mike has a blood clot in his left thigh—nothing even close to a charley horse! He will stay here for a few days to get the thickness of his blood regulated again before returning to therapy.

FEBRUARY 15

We are back at the rehab facility and the evening shift has begun. A different nurse is here and has asked about Mike's story, When I tell the part about Mike's leg pain and the incorrect diagnosis, she looks at us and says,

"You know you can change doctors, don't you?"

Perhaps we entertained an angel unawares that night …. We never saw her again, but thanks to her, we were given another doctor who was very attentive to what was happening with Mike's blood clots and helped speed his recovery.

FEBRUARY 16

We need God to do something else big, and not just with Mike's health. The cost of his medical expenses are already mounting, and while we have health insurance, there are many deductibles and co-pays that need to be taken care of—expenses that we don't have the means to pay. The emergency care, so many days in ICU, the rehab, surgeries: all of these add up to astronomical costs. We are not strangers to God's provision. The Lord has carried us through many times of perceived lack, and this time I know he will hold us close again.

✦ ✦ ✦

One miraculous time, Church Alive! had been asked to leave our rented building, and a couple close to our hearts—Chuck and Lissa—were repeatedly prodded by the Lord to help finance a building of our own. They ended up providing the entire amount needed for phase one of a building on a ten-acre site, with the agreement the church would pay them back one-quarter of it to a foundation that helps build other churches. God so miraculously used an obedient couple willing to obey his prompting to help us begin to fulfill the vision given us—for all of us to be alive in Christ and alive for others at Church Alive!

✦ ✦ ✦

And so God has provided for us again. Our family—the members of our church we love as our own—have taken up a collection. It covers most of the expenses the insurance won't cover. There is something about receiving such a huge gift of love that softens my heart to mush and makes my lower lip tremble all day.

I've always held that it's much easier to give than to receive, because receiving indicates need and, in our culture, need indicates failure. I never think about that when I'm on the giving end though. It always causes my heart to burst with joy at seeing someone's needs met in a practical way, in a way that demonstrates the heart of our Father.

To do anything other than receive with a joyful heart is to cut off the joy of the giver, and I have no intention of stopping the outpouring of love for Mike and me.

FEBRUARY 20

Sarah had her baby girl today! It's hard to put into words how it feels to be a grandmother, to be in the delivery room and witness the beginning of a new circle of life.

Only the God of all creation could plan every detail of a birth so precisely. To this day, I don't understand how people can experience the birth of a baby and not believe in God.

My role as mother has now morphed into something richer. You forget about the tiny hands and fingernails. Yes, you hold other people's babies and you are filled with wonder and gratitude at how God brings it all to delivery, but when you hold your own ....

Sarah is doing well, and Jason has been an incredible labor coach. Baby Michelle Bailey is healthy and whole. I say my goodbyes after a sleepless but unforgettable night, for all three of us. I smell her baby skin one last time before heading back to Mike with the photos in my phone.

FEBRUARY 22

And two days later, thanks to Paulette holding down the fort at the hospital, I am holding another bundle wrapped in a soft pink towel. She's barely an hour old and was *not* impressed with her first bath.

I can feel the changing winds, the earth becoming solid under my feet again. Shaun and Meghan's daughter, Drew, will take her place in life and build a legacy of her own, just as Mike and I have done. Thank you, Jesus!

These few days of sitting and rocking new life refill my soul with strength and joy, and I leave refueled and ready for God's next victory.

FEBRUARY 23

The doctors have found another blood clot in Mike's groin area. Once again, I have the opportunity to come against fear and believe and speak that, according to God's Word, Mike is whole and healed....

It's only a few hours later and already Mike is cleared to use a walker and put weight on his left leg. I think he's itching to see his new granddaughters, and no clot is going to stop him!

MARCH 10 2010

It's been a long, obstacle-filled road, but this is the day. Today! Mike has been working hard for the last two weeks to get as much physical function back as he can, both in his legs and speech, and the staff is satisfied that he is on the road to normal living.

Mike is in the car and we are on our way home. And we pull out to the edge of the parking lot where the street meets the lines of cars, and I find it hard to swallow or see for a moment. We are together again, filled with hope for the future and a deeper faith than ever. I turn to him and put my hand over his and hold it there.

And then I take the wheel again and swing out onto the street that will take us home.

THE BLESSING OF LIFE

SARAH & JASON'S FAMILY

SHAUN & MEGHAN'S FAMILY

12

EPILOGUE

SHERI

It has been five years since Mike's ski accident. In some ways it seems like it never happened and in others, it's like it was only ten minutes ago. Looking back, I am reminded of God's faithfulness to his Word and the power in it. I am also reminded of his amazing grace that was working in me to be able to stand in faith despite the life-threatening situation my husband faced. Despite my few emotional meltdowns, I knew I could depend on God and his words during every bit of that journey.

MIKE

I don't remember much of that time in my life. Right before the accident, we were on the slopes having a good time. The snow was good and we were enjoying our time together, talking and taking in all the beauty of the snowcapped mountains. On our second or third run, Shaun was snowboarding through the trees and I was keeping up with him by skiing in that narrow space on the run next to the tree line—one of my favorite places to ski because the snow is fresher there. It's easier to keep your skis close together and you can move with greater speed.

I was trying to keep close to Shaun when I was suddenly cut off and had to take a sharp left, which instantly caught my skis in the deeper snow. I couldn't maneuver them properly and, still going at full speed, I hit a tree about 12-15 inches wide. Shaun said it was like I was folded up against the tree when he got to me.

I remember a woman trying to get me to repeat my favorite color to keep me from blacking out. Things seemed to fade in and out and I was in excruciating pain. I instinctively put my right hand over my left rib cage and started praying. The EMT was asking, "What is he saying?" Shaun told her I was saying the name of Jesus. A few minutes later I was praying in tongues and she said to Shaun, "What is he doing now?" He said that I was praying in tongues and she told Shaun, "I've never heard anyone pray like that before."

I only remember a few things after that. I remember the ride down the mountain and being driven to the hospital. The guy was driving really fast, and every time he went around yet another curve on the mountainous road, the pain was excruciating. I had cracked three of the same ribs many years before this accident—when I was thirteen—but the pain didn't seem comparable at all. We were later to learn that I had eight broken ribs on that side. On the ride, and going into the ER, I held my left arm up with my right hand. It seemed to help the pain and help my breathing.

The last thing I remember was Sheri letting the doctor cut off my new ski pants, after which I was out of the conscious realm for four weeks. During that time I had many dreams running through my mind, and in many of the scenes I felt like I was dying and that those taking care of me were letting me die. Note: These were my *feelings* and inner visions, but at times God helped me respond with declarations of faith (see p 34).

I was much more aware of my surroundings the day they moved me to the trach hospital in Albuquerque. I remember being strapped down on the gurney in the ambulance, feeling very scared and humbled. Feeling the speed the driver was going at and seeing how many things around me were rattling in the vehicle only compounded my fear and awareness of my total helplessness—I couldn't move or speak and had no strength to do anything should an accident have happened. It raised the awareness of my dependency on the Lord and others for my total care.

I wasn't necessarily used to being told what to do from morning 'til night, but I gradually accepted that I had to do whatever I was told. I had a bad habit of staying up late, but the nurses got on me about that. I got frustrated easily with little things, like the air mattress constantly losing so much air I was lying on hard metal, and lying in beds that were too small for me. In addition, I could not communicate easily with my family, and my pain meds were being reduced.

I look back now and am amazed at Sheri and how she acted throughout the whole recovery period. I have so much appreciation for her faith, her discipline, her dedication to fight for me in prayer. I truly don't believe I would have survived had it not been for her prayers and declarations over me.

I used to be the strong one in the family, and I know this has had a much more emotional impact on the whole family than it has had on me. The family took over and became my strength. That has humbled me in many ways. I liked being the one who looked after everyone else, and it was hard at times to be the helpless one on the receiving end of love.

I went back to the rehab for therapy regularly for three more weeks. I wasn't supposed to drive, but Sheri told me it was time! She was copping an attitude with me, and she let me know that it was time to get with the program. My thinking was that I'd like to have been babied for a little longer, but she said that if I was healed, then why did I need to be babied? It was a good thing she did, or my recovery would have taken even longer. It took so much effort to walk up a few steps or get into the bathtub, and even these days I can be very happy about just being able to do that and a lot of other little things.

Sometimes I asked myself why certain things were still continuing, but recognized that many times I had floated along with the program rather than done the things I was supposed to do. I had a responsibility to keep building and acting on my faith and to do all the physical exercises I'd been given. Things had been normal for so many years that I had to kick into fight mode and "get 'er done."

That year, I surprised everyone and preached at church the Sunday before Easter. My speech wasn't back to normal—I sounded like a stroke victim at first—but within two months people were able to understand me better. The emotional impact my healing has had on people has been powerful, for some more than others. I've been called a walking miracle.

These days I have certain residual issues from the accident. I still have to elevate my legs at night so they don't swell, and my ribcage is a little deformed. Sometimes I'll catch my breath when I twist a certain way, but now I can move my damaged arm fully again. Overall I'd say I have about 80 percent of my original fitness level back, which is incredible when you consider my story.

I know that during all this my wonderful and faithful wife, family, and church family were standing in faith and prayer, and that is what turned my situation around; it made all the difference. I am so thankful for everyone who prayed and all the goodness and grace of our precious Lord Jesus Christ, our loving Father, and the powerful help of the Holy Spirit.

I've found I have more empathy for people since my rapid encounter with that tree. I understand why people might move slowly, and it doesn't irritate me anymore. I'm more patient in many ways, and I have a lot more compassion for people in pain. Our story has encouraged many people who go through hard times, and it comforts them.

I appreciate Sheri even more. One of the many advantages to being married for a long time is that you go through so many different seasons together. I got to see her in a new light that year. Family time is also richer, and I continuously feel thankful for still being here to enjoy this next generation. I feel an urgent sense of responsibility to teach and model faith and relationship with God in order to equip our growing family for daily life. I don't want Christ to merely be a statement of belief for them, but a constant presence in their minds and hearts.

We've been on a few mission trips since the accident. My doctor was concerned about my blood possibly clotting on the long flights, but my trust is in God and I have a filter in place that's supposed to catch them. Also,

I'm a bit stubborn…. Hopefully that stubbornness or determination is projected toward the right things and good outcomes. We're both radical about healing, but I still make sure I eat well and get regular checkups. By faith I'm healed, but I'm also going to do what I need to do in the natural realm to stay healthy.

Receiving God's grace and acting in faith works, and God honors us with his strength.

I've been stirring myself up even more lately. I want to go beyond a comfortable life and continue to train leaders to reach their full potential and help the youth at Church Alive! become disciplined world influencers. Reaching this point is due to a combination of things—getting older, psychological changes, growing grandchildren, my mom dying … mortality in general. During my recovery from the accident, I didn't focus much on dying, but on living. Growing older shifts the focus back.

Sheri and I are still building a legacy that (hopefully) has substance. Our faith has increased and is more secure. We are more confident in our prayers. We are more stirred up to see healings and have seen more people healed in our church services.

These days I mostly think about how we're all on a journey. This is not just our story; it's the story of many people who have faced the fire and walked through it with Jesus. Every moment is important because he's in it. Every moment gives us the opportunity for a testimony. I'll leave you with this key to living well:

SEEK HIS KINGDOM FIRST.

ENJOY THIS LIFE YOU'VE BEEN GIVEN.

IMPACT THE LIVES AROUND YOU.

FAITH DEVELOPED

Mike and I didn't start our faith walk with the accident. Our faith has developed over many years, and we have learned that faith comes by hearing God's Word, but faith is released through speaking God's Word. Faith is in two places: our hearts and our mouths. This journey of faith that started so many years ago continues on in our lives.

By faith we received Jesus Christ as our Lord and Savior.

> Romans 10:9-10 - If you confess with your mouth the Lord Jesus and believe in your heart that God has raised Him from the dead, you will be saved. For with the heart one believes unto righteousness, and with the mouth confession is made unto salvation.

By faith we received the infilling of the Holy Spirit.

> Acts 2:4 - And they were all filled with the Holy Spirit and began to speak with other tongues, as the Spirit gave them utterance.

By faith we tithe on our income and also give offerings according to God's Word.

> Malachi 3:10 - "Bring all the tithes into the storehouse,

that there may be food in My house, and try Me now in this," says the Lord of hosts, "If I will not open for you the windows of heaven and pour out for you such blessing that there will not be room enough to receive it.

By faith we believe for healing for ourselves, our families, and others in the body of Christ on an ongoing basis.

Mark 16:18 - They will take up serpents; and if they drink anything deadly, it will by no means hurt them; they will lay hands on the sick, and they will recover.

By faith we serve in and attend our local church.

Hebrews 10:24-25 - And let us consider one another in order to stir up love and good works, not forsaking the assembling of ourselves together, as is the manner of some, but exhorting one another, and so much the more as you see the Day approaching.

By faith we believed for a boy and a girl.

Psalms 37:4 — Delight yourself also in the Lord, and He shall give you the desires of your heart.

By faith we trained and taught our children to live by faith and not fear.

Hebrews 11:6 — But without faith it is impossible to please Him, for he who comes to God must believe that He is, and that He is a rewarder of those who diligently seek Him.

2 Timothy 1:7 — For God has not given us a spirit of fear, but of power and of love and of a sound mind.

By faith we believed to start our own construction company.

Psalm 1:3 — He shall be like a tree planted by the rivers of water, that brings forth its fruit in its season, whose leaf also shall not wither; and whatever he does shall prosper.

By faith we believed for a new home.

> Matthew 6:33 — But seek first the kingdom of God and His righteousness, and all these things shall be added to you.

By faith we attended Rhema Bible Training Center.

> Luke 14:27 — And whoever does not bear his cross and come after Me cannot be My disciple.

By faith we believed for income while attending Bible school.

> Luke 6:38 — Give, and it will be given to you: good measure, pressed down, shaken together, and running over will be put into your bosom. For with the same measure that you use, it will be measured back to you.

By faith we served on a church staff team for ten years, after attending Bible school.

> Romans 8:14 — For as many as are led by the Spirit of God, these are sons of God.

By faith we believed for college tuition.

> Philippians 4:19 — And my God shall supply all your need according to His riches in glory by Christ Jesus.

By faith we started Church Alive! on Albuquerque's west side.

> Romans 8:14 — For as many as are led by the Spirit of God, these are sons of God.

By faith we believed for two million dollars to purchase land and a building.

> Ephesians 3:20 — Now to Him who is able to do exceedingly abundantly above all that we ask or

think, according to the power that works in us.

By faith we believed for our children's spouses, weddings, and our grandchildren.

> Deuteronomy 7:13 — And He will love you and bless you and multiply you; He will also bless the fruit of your womb and the fruit of your land.

> Deuteronomy 8:18 — And you shall remember the Lord your God, for it is He who gives you power to get wealth, that He may establish His covenant which He swore to your fathers, as it is this day.

By faith we stood and believed for Mike to live and not die.

> Psalm 118:17 — I shall not die, but live, and declare the works of the Lord.

By faith we believe to build many churches in Thailand (four to date) and give regularly to mission projects.

> Mark 16:15 — And He said to them, "Go into all the world and preach the gospel to every creature."

By faith we believe to see people's lives changed and healed by the power of God.

> James 5:14-15 — Is anyone among you sick? Let him call for the elders of the church, and let them pray over him, anointing him with oil in the name of the Lord. And the prayer of faith will save the sick, and the Lord will raise him up. And if he has committed sins, he will be forgiven.

By faith we believe for the building expansion of our current debt-free building.

> Ephesians 3:20 — Now to Him who is able to do exceedingly abundantly above all that we ask or

think, according to the power that works in us.

Mark 9:23 — Jesus said to him, "If you can believe, all things are possible to him who believes."

By faith we believe we will add additional services at Church Alive! to impact more people.

Psalm 37:4 - Delight yourself also in the Lord, and He shall give you the desires of your heart.

By faith we call for more than enough money to cover our staff and their families' expenses and to expand our staff.

Ephesians 3:20 - Now to Him who is able to do exceedingly abundantly above all that we ask or think, according to the power that works in us.

By faith we believe for my first book, *Ten Minutes to Live,* to be a tool to impact and change thousands of people's lives, all for the glory of God.

Psalms 1:3 - He shall be like a tree, planted by the rivers of water, that brings forth its fruit in its season, whose leaf also shall not wither; and whatever he does shall prosper.

By faith we continue to serve God with all our hearts and fulfill the number of our days on the earth in health.

Exodus 23:25-26 — So you shall serve the Lord your God, and He will bless your bread and your water. And I will take sickness away from the midst of you. No one shall suffer miscarriage or be barren in your land; I will fulfill the number of your days.

Job 8:7 — Though your beginning was small, yet your latter end would increase abundantly.

I want to challenge you, the reader, to take a few minutes

to look back on your life and write your own faith chapter. That will include things God has done in the past, what he is doing now, and what you are believing to happen in the future, all based on his Word, which is his will.

What more can I do but give God glory for all he has done in our lives? There have been lots of ups and downs in our lifetime. God doesn't promise us a problem-free life, but he promises to never leave us or forsake us in the midst of them. Let us all continue on our journey by faith.

A PRAYER

FOR THOSE WHO WOULD LIKE TO KNOW JESUS

Dear Heavenly Father,

I come to you in the name of Jesus.

Your Word says, "The one who comes to Me I will by no means cast out" (John 6:37), so I know you won't cast me out. You take me in, and I thank you for it.

You said in your Word, "Whoever calls on the name of the Lord shall be saved" (Romans 10:13). I am calling on your name, so I know you have saved me now.

You also said, "If you confess with your mouth the Lord Jesus and believe in your heart that God has raised Him from the dead, you will be saved. For with the heart one believes unto righteousness, and with the mouth confession is made unto salvation" (Romans 9:9-10). I believe in my heart Jesus Christ is the Son of God. I believe that he was raised from the dead for my justification, and I confess him now as my Lord.

Because your Word says, "With the heart one believes unto righteousness," and I do believe with my heart, I have now become the righteousness of God in Christ (2 Corinthians 5:21) and I am saved!

Thank you, Lord!

MIKE'S FIRST DAY BACK AT CHURCH

MIKE & SHERI - FEBRUARY 13, 2013

MINISTRY TOGETHER

EXACTLY TWO YEARS LATER

MIKE & SHERI TODAY

A PRAYER FOR THE HURTING

Father, I pray for those reading this book who are in the midst of a hard situation. Whether the situation involves healing, finances, relationships, children, or parents, I pray that you will direct them to your Word. Your Word is your will for us and is more powerful than a two-edged sword. As they find your words of promise and believe them, they will experience your power working in them and the situations they are facing. I also pray for peace, comfort, and the grace to go through what they are facing; that they may be strong in their confidence and trust in you. I pray they would not be moved by their emotions or negative thoughts, but immovable and in faith in what your Word says about their situations. We thank you in advance for hearing our prayers, and we give you all the glory and honor, knowing it is you who turned the situation around. We believe we received those things which we prayed for in Jesus's name.

Amen

HEALING SCRIPTURES

Below is the e-mail we sent out to church members during Mike's recovery period. Feel free to insert the names of loved ones in place of ours when praying for your own loved ones.

HEALING SCRIPTURES

Church Alive!, it is important that we pray the Scriptures listed here DAILY for <u>Pastors Mike and Sheri </u>and the rest of the family. This allows us to be in agreement with each other and to corporately declare what God has stated in his Word.

Begin your prayer by saying, "Lord, I come to you thanking you for fulfilling the promises in your Word. I pray the Scriptures below according to Romans 4:17 that says, 'God speaks of the nonexistent things that [He has foretold and promised] as if they [already] existed.' By faith, I declare the following:"

FOR PASTOR MIKE

Psalm 29:11:The Lord will give [unyielding and impenetrable] strength to Pastor Mike; the Lord will bless Pastor Mike with peace.

Psalm 30:2: Lord my God, Pastor Mike cried to You and You have healed him.

Psalm 34:19: Many evils confront the [consistently] righteous, but the Lord delivers Pastor Mike out of them all.

Psalm 103:3: God forgives [every one of] Pastor Mike's iniquities, God heals [each one of] all of Pastor Mike's diseases and injuries.

Psalm 107:20: He sends forth His word and heals Pastor Mike and rescues him from the pit and destruction.

Psalm 118:17: Pastor Mike shall not die but live, and shall declare the works and recount the illustrious acts of the Lord.

Psalm 147:3: He heals the brokenhearted and binds up Pastor Mike's wounds [curing his pains and his sorrows].

Proverbs 4:20-22: Pastor Mike, attend to God's words; consent and submit to His sayings. Let them not depart from your sight; keep them in the center of your heart. For they are life to you, Pastor Mike, because you find them and healing and health to all your flesh.

Isaiah 53:4-5: Surely He has borne Pastor Mike's grief (sickness, weakness, and distress) and carried his sorrows and pains, He was wounded for Pastor Mike's transgressions, He was bruised for Pastor Mike's guilt and iniquities; the chastisement [needed to obtain] peace and well-being for Pastor Mike was upon Him, and with the stripes [that wounded] Him, Pastor Mike is healed and made whole.

Isaiah 58:8: Then shall Pastor Mike's light break forth like the morning, and his healing (his restoration and the power of a new life) shall spring forth speedily; Pastor Mike's righteousness (his rightness, his justice, and his right relationship with God) shall go before him [conducting him to peace and prosperity], and the glory of the Lord shall be Pastor Mike's rear guard.

Jeremiah 30:17: For I will restore health to Pastor Mike, and I will heal his wounds, says the Lord.

Matthew 8:13 (NIV): Then Jesus said to the Church Alive! members, "Go! It will be done just as you believed it would." And their servant, Pastor Mike, was healed at that very hour.

Romans 8:11: The Spirit of Him Who raised up Jesus from the dead dwells in Pastor Mike, He Who raised up Christ Jesus from the dead will also restore to life Pastor Mike's mortal (short-lived, perishable) body through His Spirit Who dwells in Pastor Mike.

1 Peter 2:24: He personally bore Pastor Mike's sins in His [own] body on the tree [as on an altar and offered Himself on it], that Pastor Mike might die (cease to exist) to sin and live to righteousness. By His wounds Pastor Mike has been healed.

3 John 1:2 : Beloved, I pray that Pastor Mike may prosper in every way and [that his body] may keep well, even as [I know] his soul keeps well and prospers.

Revelation 12:11 (NLT): And Pastor Mike has defeated

him (Satan) by the blood of the Lamb and by the word of <u>his</u> testimony.

FOR <u>**PASTOR SHERI**</u> AND THE FAMILY

Deuteronomy 31:6: Be strong, courageous, and firm; fear not nor be in terror before the situation, for it is the Lord God Who goes with <u>Pastor Sheri</u> and <u>her</u> family; He will not fail them or forsake them.

Isaiah 26:3: You will guard <u>Pastor Sheri</u> and <u>her</u> family and keep them in perfect and constant peace whose minds [both their inclination and their character] are stayed on You, because they commit themselves to You, lean on You, and hope confidently in You.

John 14:27: Peace I leave with <u>Pastor Sheri</u> and <u>her</u> family; My [own] peace I now give and bequeath to <u>Pastor Sheri</u> and <u>her</u> family. Not as the world gives do I give to them. Do not let their hearts be troubled, neither let them be afraid. [Stop allowing themselves to be agitated and disturbed; and do not permit themselves to be fearful and intimidated and cowardly and unsettled.]

Romans 8:37: Yet amid all these things, <u>Pastor Sheri</u> and family, you are more than conquerors and gain a surpassing victory through Him Who loved you.

2 Corinthians 2:14: But thanks be to God, Who in Christ always leads <u>Pastor Sheri</u> and <u>her</u> family in triumph [as trophies of Christ's victory] and through them spreads and makes evident the fragrance of the knowledge of God everywhere.

Philippians 4:6-7: Do not fret, <u>Pastor Sheri</u> and family members, or have any anxiety about anything, but in every circumstance and in everything, by prayer and petition (definite requests), with thanksgiving, continue to make your wants known to God. And God's peace [shall be Pastor Sheri's and her family's, that tranquil state of a soul assured of its salvation through Christ, and so fearing nothing from God and being content with its earthly lot of whatever sort that is, that peace] which transcends all understanding shall garrison and mount guard over their hearts and minds in Christ Jesus.

2 Thessalonians 3:16: Now may the Lord of peace Himself grant Pastor Sheri and her family His peace (the peace of His kingdom) at all times and in all ways [under all circumstances and conditions, whatever comes].

1 Peter 5:7: Casting the whole of their care, Pastor Sheri and family members, [all their anxieties, all their worries, all their concerns, once and for all] on Him, for He cares for them affectionately and cares about them watchfully.

All Scripture are paraphrased from the Amplified Bible, unless otherwise stated.

HEALING PRAYER

Heavenly Father, I thank you for all the promises of your Word, which proclaim healing to those who are sick. Your Word is truth,[1] and it is forever settled in heaven.[2] You tell me in your Word that you have provided healing for me through the stripes of Jesus Christ, my Lord.[3] I believe this because this is what your Word says.

Deliver me from all fear, thoughts, and imaginations the devil would bring to torment me.[4] Through faith in your Word, I now bring every thought, and all imaginations and reasonings into captivity to the obedience of Christ.[5] In the authority of the matchless name of Jesus Christ, I confront the devil, the enemy of my soul, and all related fears he attempts to assail me with, and I command him to stop his efforts against me now.[6]

This sickness has a name, Father, and your Word says that every name must bow its knee at the mere mention of the name of Jesus.[7] Therefore, Father, in the name of Jesus, through faith in that name,[8] and through the merits of the precious blood of Jesus Christ; I now command this illness of _____ in my body to bow its knee and to leave my body forever.[9] I ask you, Father, to watch over these words of faith and bring them to pass by your great power.[10]

Your Word imparts faith for healing to my heart.[11] I receive your Word, your strength, and your healing now as I pray. I know that through Jesus I have been made whole.[12] I release my faith in your Word through my words, and I say that I am whole and healed now according to your Word.[13]

By faith in your Word, I say thank you, Father, that I am healed and whole according to your Word. I will not be moved by symptoms, circumstances, or bad reports. I continually thank you and declare by Jesus's stripes I am the healed of the Lord.

1. John 17:17
2. Psalms 119:89
3. Isaiah 53:5
4. Joel 2:32
5. 2 Corinthians 10:5
6. James 4:7
7. Philippians 2:10
8. John 14:13
9. Mark 11:23
10. Jeremiah 1:12
11. Romans 10:17
12. Acts 9:34
13. Mark 11:23

Part of this prayer was taken from the book *Healing Prayers* by Clift and Kathleen Richards.

RECOMMENDED READING

There are some books you come across that you never forget, because their truths rest in your spirit forever. These books' truths live on in my spirit.

The Believer's Authority by Kenneth E. Hagin - A believer's guide to understanding the kingdom authority we have and how to use it.

God's Creative Power Gift Collection by Charles Capps - A gift set of the books *God's Creative Power Will Work for You, God's Creative Power for Healing,* and *God's Creative Power for Finances.* Learn how to put God's creative power to work through you.

Bible Study Faith Course by Kenneth E. Hagin - An in-depth Bible study on how to walk in faith and victory.

Understanding the Purpose and Power of Prayer by Dr. Myles Munroe - A biblical study on how to communicate with God and pray his perfect will.

ABOUT THE AUTHOR

Sheri Schaefer was born in Oklahoma and raised in Santa Fe, New Mexico. until her college years, when her parents moved to Albuquerque. She met her husband, Mike, while attending the University of New Mexico and later graduated with a husband and a masters degree. Today, Mike and Sheri have two adult children (who are married to amazing, loving spouses), and they adore their four grandchildren.

Sheri is passionate about teaching on parenting, marriage, and faith. She and Mike have pastored Church Alive! since 1995. When they are not pastoring they love to travel, ski, scuba dive, snorkel, hang out at the beach, and read. Taking mission trips into China and Thailand has enriched their lives and expanded their love for people.

Sheri's website

sherischaefer.com

Connect with Sheri online:

E-mail: sheriglen@gmail.com

Church Alive's website

www.churchaliveabq.com

ABOUT THE COAUTHOR

Sally Hanan was an Irish import to the US back in the '90s, along with her husband and two young children. Since then she has managed to homeschool her above average kids (who are obviously absolute geniuses and extremely good-looking), acquire more "stuff" than she knows what to do with, and spend hours on Facebook.

On a more professional note, Sally runs a writing and editing business. She has also been counseling people for about twenty years and recently became a certified life coach, because she gets bored easily and she loves fixing people as well as words.

Buy Sally's books on Amazon:

Joy in a Box - A collection of flash fiction

Fix Yourself in Jesus - A step-by-step guide to inner healing for individuals and groups

Empower Yourself in the Holy Spirit - A step-by-step guide to the use of the gifts of the Spirit for individuals and groups

Sally's websites:

Writing and editing services:
inksnatcher.com

Coaching & counseling services:
morethanbreathing.com

Connect with Sally online:

E-mail: inkmeister@inksnatcher.com

Facebook: Inksnatcher

www.ingramcontent.com/pod-product-compliance
Lightning Source LLC
Chambersburg PA
CBHW070545090426
42735CB00013B/3076